Galley

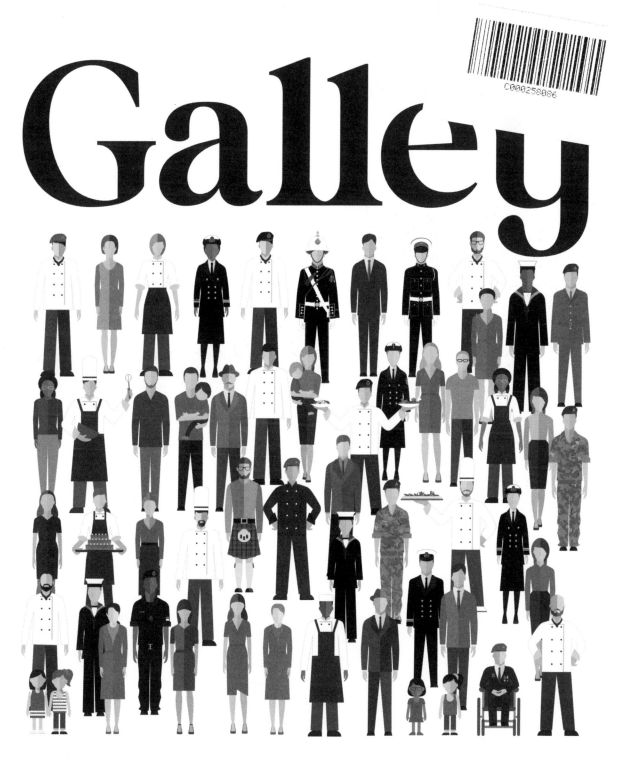

THE ROYAL NAVY & ROYAL MARINES CHARITY COOKBOOK

ROYAL NAVY & ROYAL MARINES CHARITY

C000258086

Acknowledgements

This book is the brainchild of Mattie Tew and he would like to thank the following people without whom this book would never have made it to the shelves:

To Mattie's wife, Lauran, and family for everything they do to support him, always.

To Bob Field for being an all-round bon oeuf, as well as for listening to the kernel of an idea and helping to bring it to life. He's simply the best.

To Adrian Bell, CEO of the RNRMC for believing in this project and allowing us to pursue it.

To Dawn Ingram, for making all this possible.

To ESS Defence and The Compass Group for supporting the RNRMC and giving the book its full backing.

To HRH The Princess Royal for being kind enough to write the foreword and for continually supporting the RNRMC and Naval Service.

To Meze Publishing who have been patient and understanding throughout and have produced a book beyond our expectations.

To the talented chefs who kindly contributed to the production of the book; it is nothing without you.

To Essential Cuisine and their continued support in supplying Royal Naval Units with outstanding products with great-tasting, easy-to-use stocks and sauce bases, making galley life that little bit easier.

To the daughter of Arthur William Hayne, Julie, and Rear Admiral Terry Loughran for showing us a glimpse of our past.

To Warrant Officer Trevor Llewellyn MBE for his contribution and introducing Mattie to the RNRMC.

To Warrant Officer Tony Shelley and Jason Deane for their contributions and supporting Mattie with top cover.

To all Mattie's colleagues at the Food Services Training Squadron, MOD Worthy Down.

"The Royal Navy chefs' course must be the hardest course in the world because nobody's ever passed it."

CONTENTS

RECIPES & CHEFS

Foreword

More than simply nutrition, food and drink have always played a central role in life in the Royal Navy. By the 1790s and early 1800s, the Royal Navy was providing rations for over 100,000 men, with no refrigeration, modern preservatives or packaging. Contrary to popular myth, the diet of sailors in the Royal Navy in Nelson's time was both plentiful and good quality, averaging out at over 5,000 calories each day, thanks to Admiral Duncan. Phrases such as 'piping hot', from when a piped signal indicated hot food was available in the galley, and 'square meal', from the square plates on which sailors' food was served, have now expanded from their origins in Naval galleys into our everyday language.

Mealtimes continue to play an important part in Navy life and are often a key component in the morale of a busy warship, for example preparing to go on, or coming off, watch or duty. They also act as important markers of days of the week – for instance, fish and chips on a Friday – or the time of day, and not just on submarines inhabiting a world without daylight. Special meals in the Royal Navy also commemorate important maritime victories such as at Trafalgar and Taranto, with demonstrations of expert culinary skill and fine dining. But, above all, meals bring people together and encourage a sense of camaraderie and belonging, which is so vital to harmonious living in the confined quarters of a warship at sea.

Strangely, until 1806 the only qualification required to become a ship's cook (as opposed to a Captain's cook), was to be a Greenwich Chest pensioner, and these men were often missing limbs. Ship's cooks had no formal culinary training, instead acquiring their skills through experience. Nowadays, the Royal Navy Catering specialisation expertly trains and produces chefs of the highest calibre, who are able to produce the recipes detailed on these pages. They work often in the smallest of galleys or field kitchens, under the most demanding conditions, with a resourcefulness and flair, which – when paired with the hospitality for which the Royal Navy is justly renowned – makes for a truly winning combination.

All the proceeds from the sale of this collection of recipes will go towards supporting all those who serve in the Royal Navy, regardless of specialisation, and who gave their service in the past, and of course their families who may need help today. The nation makes extraordinary demands on each and every member of the Royal Navy and by extension, a forward deployed and global Royal Navy invariably places greater strain on family relationships. By purchasing this book you will experience a range of excellent meals and help the Royal Navy and Royal Marines Charity to provide lifelong support to all those who serve in Her Majesty's Royal Navy.

For those of us who take a day or two to acclimatize, the spicy option often works – ginger biscuits or cake, spicy roasted squash and pepper soup, a mild curry or marmite sandwiches!

HRH The Princess Royal, Patron of the Royal Navy and Royal Marines Charity

A note from our Platinum Partner ESS

Food is a powerful thing. Not only does it fuel us, but it brings us together. It supports social interaction, the building of relationships and the making of memories, whether over a formal meal, a bite to eat at lunch, or a drink and a snack in the evening.

At ESS, food service is our heritage. We have fed military personnel for over 70 years, from day to day catering in messes and packed meals sustaining those out on exercise to regular mess functions and VIP events. We are passionate about delivering great dining experiences whenever and wherever our customers require them.

The creation of enticing, exciting dishes is something our chefs pride themselves on, and we are thrilled to sponsor this project, which we hope will inspire others to do the same – you will even spot recipes from some of our ex-Royal Navy chefs featured in the pages. I'm looking forward to trying out some of the recipes myself, although I can't guarantee that the presentation will be quite as impressive!

We feel privileged to have a longstanding working relationship with the Royal Navy and Royal Marines Charity, and to play a part in the great work the organisation does for serving and former sailors, marines and their families. The Royal Navy and Royal Marines Charity Cookbook has afforded us the fantastic opportunity to combine support for the charity with what we enjoy best – great food! Enjoy!

Mark Webster

Managing Director, ESS

(ESS is the Defence, Energy & Government Services sector of Compass Group UK & Ireland)

Why we made this book

To me, cooking in the Royal Navy can go a couple of ways: you either turn up, open a box and heat food up; or you could have a real sense of passion for your job, and every meal you serve is better than the last.

There is the well-known saying within the Royal Navy that 'there are 240 chefs onboard a ship and the worst nine are the ones who end up in the galley'. To some that is an insult, to me that is a challenge.

Before I joined the Royal Navy, starting out as a young man, I had a passion for cooking, I wasn't the best, however I had a willingness to learn and that goes a long way. When I told people I was joining the Royal Navy as a chef, they would often say, "some of the best chefs in the world have had Naval training". It wasn't everyone's reaction though, because at school I didn't really listen or even attend most days. My head of year always said I'd never go anywhere in life and I was a non-achiever. That has always stuck with me throughout my career – and it gives me fire in my belly to go and do my best.

Now you'll always get your haters and you'll always get your very own Michelin-starred chefs as part of any Ship's Company, who will complain about absolutely anything to do with the food onboard.

Cooking for the masses isn't always glamorous; you don't always have the best ingredients and you don't always have the equipment that works. However, over my years in the Royal Navy, whether it be at sea in a Type 42 destroyer, the middle of Afghanistan or simply alongside in base port, I truly believe that it isn't about kit or ingredients, but about the passion a person has for their job and their industry.

A lot has changed since I joined up and it will continue to change. You will also get chefs that have been before me and say: "It wasn't like that in my day on the Massive," but we are in a job of trends that change on a weekly basis. Cooking is cooking, people have their own ways, trends, styles, skillsets, etc. and everyone is different. We might not do things the same anymore, but the industry is forever evolving.

The chefs within the Royal Navy and Royal Marines find themselves in their own war, except it's not fought with the ammunition, bombs and rockets that we hold in our magazines, but with the service of food and beverages. Laugh as you may at my last statement, with the Royal Navy and Royal Marines deployed around the globe, there is a major call for Defence engagement.

Foreign ministers, Members of Parliament and occasionally members of the Royal Family will use Naval vessels, and acting on behalf of the British sovereign, they conduct important meetings that could end with peace deals and sometimes even stop conflicts and political arguments. Therefore, it is our job as chefs to cater for such high-profile events; and if the food leaves a positive lasting impression on the people attending, then we have played a big part.

I soon realised that, as a chef onboard, my resources are very limited. I wanted to produce our very own reference book, so that people could see what we are capable of. We aren't the ones that open boxes, but, in fact, we are the ones that instil passion in our subordinates in our ever-evolving trade.

Within this book, you'll find some of the Royal Navy's finest culinary artists and chefs from past and present. I wanted them to take you on a journey through their time of serving within the best Navy in the world. This recipe book will capture things they have learnt who have come before me and for those who have left the service, I wanted to show you what and how they have contributed and where they are now.

The Royal Navy and Royal Marines Charity is a big part of what we all believe in. The way that they help serving personnel, veterans and their families is a gift that keeps on giving. It was our turn to give back to them. All the proceeds of this book will go to the charity, so that they can continue doing an extraordinary job.

It has been an absolute pleasure working with the charity and our sponsors Compass Group UK, who have been as ever supportive and an integral part in helping get this book together.

But my biggest thanks are to my inspiring shipmates (some mentors), past and present who have given up their own time to contribute to this great cause.

Which leaves me to say enjoy, be creative, make the recipes your own, chop and change things around, remember everyone is different and everyone has their own style. Thank you to all that have purchased this book and have supported the Royal Navy and Royal Marines Charity.

Leading Chef Mattie Tew
Royal Navy

The Royal Navy and Royal Marines Charity

The Royal Navy is both central to Britain's past and critical to its future. We estimate that some 750,000 people either wear the uniform today, have a proud history of service, or provide the bedrock of support at home.

The Royal Navy and Royal Marines Charity is proud to be the inheritor of centuries of tradition of charitable support to those who serve at sea and those who gave honourable service in the past. As the principal charity of the Royal Navy, we have a single mission: to value and support every sailor, marine and Royal Navy family, for life.

Since our formation in 2007, we have funded projects and facilities that boost morale and improve the quality of life for those who serve today. We also partner annually with approaching 60 different organisations and military and civilian charities to deliver bespoke support for Royal Navy families and children, conscious that although one person may join, the whole family in effect ends up serving. Our focus in the veteran community is centred on promoting independence and protecting dignity in old age, as well as doing all we can to facilitate the transition of working age veterans into new realms of employment.

We have worked hard to build a funding framework that has the best impact on serving personnel, the veteran community, their families and dependents at any stage of their lives. We place great focus on understanding need, early intervention and prevention so that issues do not escalate down the line. Our seven Funding Programmes, each one focusing on a beneficiary group or community, require us to work in partnership with many specialist third-sector and civilian organisations, commissioning and delivering

ground-breaking and comprehensive services, which address areas of need arising from the findings of our Need Report, published in 2018.

We are very conscious that when you consider the huge numbers of beneficiaries that the Royal Navy and Royal Marines Charity is here to support, then it is very likely that there are a significant number who need our support, but are unaware of the help that exists for them or who are reluctant to seek help. While membership of the Royal Navy community bestows many benefits, such as discipline, leadership and teamwork, many elements of military life can increase vulnerability to loneliness and social isolation. These include a mobile lifestyle, periods of separation from loved ones, and key transitions such as deployment and final discharge from service. A particular focus of our current work is to establish how best to identify and connect vulnerable veterans through support services, comradeship and improved communications with family and friends. We are currently working with Sparko TV on a pilot project involving 200 Royal Navy veterans, who are supplied with an easy-to-use device connected to their television sets, which provides them with unlimited video calling to family and friends and specially curated content to appeal to their interests.

We are also building on the findings of our Need Report to better understand and identify the gaps and overlaps in service provision across the naval charity sector to produce a blueprint for holistic welfare support, in partnership with fellow military charities, as well as others, including state departments. The overarching aim is to move the naval charity sector from reactive assistance to proactive, holistic support that focuses on prevention and early intervention

across all segments of our beneficiary family.

We have worked with a record number of charity partners over the course of the past year to improve the quality of life for all those who serve and their families, as well as promoting independence wherever we can among our veteran community. The Royal Navy is championed by a range of naval charities, each with their own specific area of support. Our collective aim is to cooperate and collaborate as closely as possible so that together we can best meet the need of our beneficiaries. In particular, all naval charities are focused on working together to tackle missed and unmet need.

The context that we are working in may have changed completely in the wake of Covid-19, but our commitment to support every serving and veteran sailor, marine and their dependents remains undiminished. The fact that there has been no disruption to our grants programme in this period is testimony to the enduring kindness and munificence of all those who support us in so many different ways, including, of course, our Platinum Bridge Partner ESS Defence who have generously underwritten all the costs associated with producing this unique volume of recipes. Their support means that 100% of the proceeds from the sale of each copy goes directly to delivering the life-long support that our beneficiaries count on us to provide.

Adrian Bell
Chief Executive,
Royal Navy and Royal Marines Charity

Catering in the Royal Navy:
a brief history

The history of chefs serving within the Royal Navy is as dark as some of the deepest recesses of a submariner's freezer. Nobody really knows when the first cooks braved the sea, but it is known that many of the first chefs were men (sorry ladies, it was all rum, bum and 'baccy' back then), who were either too old or had other job-restrictive war wounds (missing limbs etc). Indeed, the oddly named Ny Coep, the chef whose skeleton was found on King Henry VIII's flagship the Mary Rose (1510-1545), was believed to have served as a gunner who had been job-changed to the galley (ship's kitchen), due to having work-related 'dodgy' knees, ironically a common complaint in today's Navy to avoid sea time! I have no doubt that poor old Ny could pack a decent cannon with shot, but I'm willing to bet his Bloody Mary Foam starter was a little different from today's fare! In fact, no formal culinary training was required to do the job until 1806. The only professional requirement was that they had to have contributed to the Chatham Pension Chest (the RN version of the Chelsea Pensioners).

The ability to cook well was probably secondary to those 'old hands' that could soak up the food complaints and 'feed the masses' in such a way that the ship's company remained fit to fight. That said, even back then it was recognised that food (or victuals) was a vital component in a sailor's life. The famous diarist and one-time Royal Navy employee Samuel Pepys even wrote on its importance:

'seamen love their bellies above everything else … make any abatement from them in the quantity or agreeableness of the victuals, is to … provoke them in the tenderest spot' and 'render them disgusted with the King's service than any … other hardship'.

He also wrote in 1677 of a sailor's ration which included:

1lb of biscuit and 1 gallon of beer daily, with a weekly ration of 8lb of beef, or 4lb of beef and 2lb of bacon or pork, with 2 pints of peas.

You may balk or perhaps smile at the beer ration but remember beer was far safer to drink in those days than water, due to the brewing process. Well, that's our excuse anyway!

The main problem of catering in this age was how to stop the food from spoiling, as well as the dreaded disease scurvy, which was caused by a lack of vitamin C. Before the age of refrigeration, perishables like meat and fish were stored in salt barrels which rendered them inedible unless the next day's ration was soaked overnight with frequent water changes to remove the salt content. The dried peas also needed soaking for several hours to reconstitute them. A favourite part of the rations was an unleavened mixture of flour, water and salt, which was premade ashore to form 'hard tack' biscuits, which the sailors soaked in their broth until their pre-NHS dentistry teeth could cope with the concrete-like texture. Scurvy was a major problem on ships and it is a popular Naval belief that scran (our word for a meal) was an acronym formed from a daily issue of Sultanas, Currants, Raisins And Nuts to stave off this horrible disease. Fresh fruit in particular was a rarity and usually only bought from hawkers' boats that came alongside to sell their wares whilst the ships were at anchor near friendly ports.

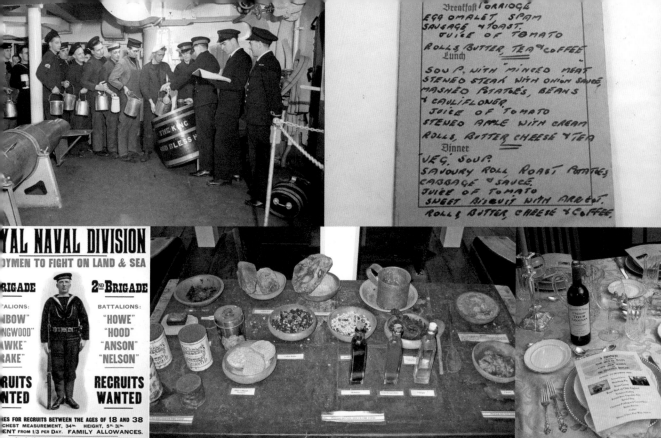

As the British Empire grew, scurvy naturally increased as ships stayed at sea longer to reach these far-flung outposts. By the late 18th century, the Admiralty was importing lemons from Europe to add their juice to the sailors' daily rum ration, which reportedly had the desired effect. I doubt the sailors even noticed the nutritional benefits after scuppering their daily ½ pint of rum! When it was realised that our own colonies grew limes (as well as making the rum) the fruit was changed for the cheaper, but admittedly less vitamin-rich, option. The still-famous brand of Rose's lime juice was set up to supply the Fleet, resulting in Americans referring to British Sailors as lime juicers, which was subsequently shortened to 'Limeys'. This use of lemon or limes in the sailors' grog may also explain the Officers' timeless debate on whether to have one or the other in their gin and tonic!

Food onboard remained largely the same for the 16th and 17th centuries – sailors have always been somewhat averse to change. Sundays, Tuesdays and Thursdays were meat days and on the remaining days they were served fish with 2 ounces of butter and 4 ounces of cheese. From 1733 to the mid-19th century, the fish rations were replaced with oatmeal and sugar. This allowed a rather repetitive daily meal intake of around 5000 Kcal, but the extremely hard manual work meant that you didn't see many chubby chaps on the decks.

The wonderfully named 'Jack Nasty Face', a battle of Trafalgar Veteran, reported his usual meals consisted of:

Breakfast	Lunch	Supper
Burgoo, made of coarse oatmeal and water or 'scotch coffee', which is burnt bread boiled in some water, and sweetened with sugar.	(the main meal of the day) Lobscouse, a typical dinner time dish, consisted of boiled salted meat, onions and pepper mixed with ship's biscuit and stewed together.	Usually a half pint of wine, or a pint of grog with biscuit and cheese or butter.

Throughout history sailors have thoroughly enjoyed critiquing the food on offer; it's often their only escape from their daily routine. Even Captain Cook used to get exasperated with their reluctance to embrace culinary change:

"Every innovation … to the advantage of seamen is sure to meet with their highest disapprobation. Both portable soup and sauerkraut were at first condemned as stuff unfit for human beings … It has been in great measure owing to various little deviations from established practice that I have been able to preserve my people from that dreadful distemper, scurvy."

There is often a misconception that Officers have always enjoyed far better rations than the ratings that served them. The fact that Captains often employed their own cooks and purchased their own additional supplementary items from their own wages is often overlooked. They were actually issued the same rations as the men, but usually had the financial means to enhance their meals to Gentlemanly standards and they were expected to take their own personal crockery onboard.

In the 18th and 19th centuries, ships would also carry livestock as a source of fresh meat and dairy. Cattle, pigs, goats and poultry were carried on board. One Royal Naval ship sailed to the East Indies in 1746 with a goat, sheep, sow, 78 hens and 13 ducks on board. Sailors also fished to supplement their diet. Sharks, flying fish, dolphins, porpoises and turtles were regularly caught and eaten. Birds including seagulls were also fair game. Rats were not exactly safe either, as sailors considered it sport to chase down the pests, skin and cook them, referring to the meat as "nice and delicate…..full and as good as rabbits".

With the dawning of the Victorian era, the first civilian 'celebrity' cooks began to emerge in society, and cooking became far more recognised as a desirable skill rather than a necessity. The developing world was blessed with chefs such as Catherine Beecher, Sarah Hale, Alexis Soyer, Charles Francatelli, Eliza Acton, Isobella Beeton and my personal favourite, Fannie Farmer. Consequently, the Admiralty who were acquainted with these developments, and whose wives and servants may have even read some these celebrity cookbooks, decided that Naval chefs should receive basic culinary training, and thereafter standards slowly improved.

Developments over the next hundred years then centred around the successful inventions of refrigeration and canning. By the First World War, the Navy had bulk refrigerated ships to carry supplies to support our fleet, but unfortunately these ships proved to be a prize target for the early German U boats.

Ships by now always carried fruit and vegetables, which were obviously used first before they deteriorated. Beef stew was still the favourite dish next to roast mutton. The canning process was by now widely used and ships could extend their endurance by storing tons of canned meat and vegetables. Corned 'bully' beef was a favourite, as well as tinned sardines and pilchards. Treats even included fruitcake, but the traditional hard tack biscuits were still a staple part of the sailors' diet and still required 'much dipping in the tea' to render them edible.

Little had changed prior to the onset of the Second World War, except in the natural developments of refrigeration. A typical daily menu on the battleship HMS King George V consisted of:

Breakfast	Dinner	Tea	Supper
Bacon and egg	Tomato soup, roast pork, potatoes, cabbage, apricots and custard	Meat paste	Lettuce, beetroot, salmon, coffee

By the 1970s, the main problem with feeding the ship's companies was a lack of money allowed by the government to feed them. Although the chefs now enjoyed advanced culinary skills, they were shackled to using cheaper cuts of meat and offal. This culminated in a decade of imaginative recipes that were surprisingly popular. On special occasions such as mess dinners you couldn't stray too far away from a prawn cocktail, steak and black forest gateaux, but the average sailor was eating the delights of 'shit on a raft' (kidneys on toast) or the up-market version; 'shit on a raft with guard rails' (kidneys on toast with mashed potato piped around the edge). Stuffed sheep's hearts, oxtails, and fried liver and onions were on the menu most weeks. I used to cry with laughter at stories of how these master craftsmen fed the fleet solely with their clever invention and adaptability. Cornflakes could bolster mince dishes and anchovy essence would disguise mashed potato powder as fish cutlets.

I have no qualms in telling you how I giggled watching new customers' faces dig into their Chinese beef dishes to find it was actually sliced liver. Tinned rations were still vital to extend the time a ship could stay at sea, and the undisputed all-time favourite dish was 'babies' heads'. You have to imagine a 7.5cm 'tube' of suet packed with the tenderest steak and kidney sat on its end, with the top open, in a rich gravy. Despite many old sailors telling you it was because they had a soft top like a new-born baby's head, it was actually because toilets in the Navy are called 'heads' and they resembled a baby's potty, hence the name... I'm afraid the Navy still enjoys toilet humour! Another favourite was (and still is) the timeless 'cheesy hammy eggy'. I will leave it to the guys contributing to this book to decide whether to reveal the 'secret' recipe. For the traditionalists, we also still carried large tins of 'ship's biscuits', which by now are losing their popularity.

I myself joined up in the early 80s. I remember standing in awe in the RN cookery school foyer, where Princess Diana's wedding cake, which they had been asked to make, was proudly displayed. Luckily, it wasn't long before the daily allowance for food increased slightly to allow the chefs to finally show off their other skills. Back then the Royal Navy was still in the process of a food revolution, embracing different cultures and experimenting with Chinese, Indian and Italian recipes. Whilst not always popular with the 'old boys' onboard, the cooks, as always, rose to the challenge, and it is somewhat rare these days to find a traditional 'British' dish on the menu, barring the ever-popular roast dinner or British sausage. With the recent rise in vegetarian/vegan diets, together with religious requirements, healthy eating and medical-related factors, the associated challenges have never been so diverse, and our cooks have taken it all in their stride. After a steady progression of experience gained onboard ships and submarines, these dedicated professionals have often become instructors themselves and many go on to showcase their talents on the National or World Stage at various competitions, including the popular BBC MasterChef series.

A typical day's menu on a frigate/destroyer in today's Royal Navy could consist of:

Breakfast	Lunch	Dinner
Full cooked English breakfast (sausage, bacon, choice of eggs, beans, tomatoes and a rotational breakfast extra such as mushrooms or smoked haddock).	Homemade soup of the day.	Lasagne al forno with focaccia.
	Salad bar.	Hunter's chicken with bbq sauce.
Natural yoghurt and fruit compote.	Homemade pizzas, including pepperoni, bbq chicken, four cheese (v) and roasted vegetables (v).	Grilled halibut steak with lime coleslaw.
		Quorn lasagne al forno (v).
Toast and preserves.	Jacket potatoes.	Roasted paprika wedges, garlic sautéed sugar snap peas, grilled tomatoes, side salad.
Variety of cereals and muesli.	Baguettes.	
Porridge.	Fresh fruit.	Jam roly poly and custard.

WO1 Taff Llewellyn MBE

"Attitude is a little thing that makes a big difference." Winston Churchill.

Who joins the Royal Navy as a chef?

Like many youngsters, I didn't really know what I wanted to do when I left school. I didn't fancy further education at college and beyond. I wanted my own money, a car and to go on holiday with my mates. Looking back now, I lacked the maturity to make any long-lasting decisions and I still needed my parents to basically keep me alive. My friends were being employed locally in a variety of jobs and meeting up for their Friday night out. Embarrassingly I was still getting pocket money and it didn't last long in the pub. My dad had suggested the Royal Navy because it was something he'd wanted to do when he was 16 but his parents wouldn't sign the papers to allow him to join. In a totally out of character flash of inspiration, I decided that I could do that! I still remember my parents bursting out laughing when I told them what job I had applied for; I couldn't even boil water. After basic training (10 weeks) I successfully passed my trade training which these days takes just under 7 months. The trick is to be receptive and enthusiastic and soak up what the incredibly talented instructors teach you, and best of all, they paid me to be there! I was told when to get up, what to wear, go to the dentist, doctors, etc, and I was with hundreds of men and women my own age. A perfect world for an indecisive person with little direction in life. To cut a very long story short I eventually ended up as the Fleet Caterer overseeing all of the catering on Royal Navy ships and submarines, as well as trying to care for all of the chefs. I've been involved with functions for VVIP's all around the world, including most of our Royal Family, presidents, sports people and film stars. I've been to 138 countries, I've walked on the Great Wall of China,

danced with Mayan warriors in Mexico, trembled in fear on the Empire State Building, crawled through Vietcong tunnels in Vietnam, arm-wrestled Russians in Vladivostok, I've ridden a camel around the Pyramids, run away from rhinos in Kenya, I've whale watched at the poles, been greeted as a war hero by Mickey Mouse in Disneyland and I've even been honoured by the Queen. These adventures aside, I occasionally pop into my hometown local on a Friday night, where my friends still gather, arguing about whether they can afford their annual holiday to Cornwall. I still have a great laugh with them and apparently it's still my round! Not bad for a lad who left school clueless eh?

These days all Catering Service Ratings (chefs) are fully trained from scratch in both the front and rear of house roles, including the computerised accounting systems and managerial procedures that accompany the role. We are a proud all-inclusive employer and we also welcome foreign and Commonwealth applicants (subject to the Foreign Office restrictions). Candidates do not require any previous catering experience or academic qualifications to apply, but they are tested on their basic maths and English skills prior to a successful application. We accept applications from personnel from 15 years 9 months up to 39 years of age. Women are an integral part of all aspects of the Navy; I know this because I was lucky enough to marry one. The old adage of 'never trust a skinny chef' may be true, but you do need a basic level of fitness to serve in the military. The fitter you are, especially prior to basic training, the easier it is.

In my opinion, the professional training that our chefs have received since the Second World War continues to be the best in the world. Our chefs all have the proven ability to produce restaurant-standard food often in adverse situations, to a tight budget and often using challenging ingredients obtained during port visits all around the world. I would challenge any of today's celebrity chefs to cook a varied menu for 200 sailors on a Destroyer, especially during rough weather or at action stations under threat of enemy fire.

Our chefs are also unique amongst the armed forces. We alone do not have 'rear echelons' filled with non-combatants working to civilian contractors' menus. With supervision, we allow our chefs to gain confidence by experimentation, using their own recipes and menus. We are literally 'all in the same boat', so we operate as 'one ship's company', which basically means that we go to war side by side with the Warfare and the Engineering branches. (Although, to be fair we spend most of our time visiting foreign countries in shorts and flip flops with an ice-cold drink, but it doesn't sound as sexy!) That aside, and as portrayed in the Steven Segal film 'Under Siege', a chef is not just a chef. We are all trained in the use of firearms, first aid and firefighting. We can be used as armed boarding parties which can include rapid roping from helicopters, or as part of a nuclear and chemical weapon decontamination team or even manning close-range air defence weapons. As a chef on a nuclear submarine, one of your main roles is to actually drive the submarine using the 'planes' (something akin to a steering wheel). Yes, I am serious.

The head chef (Senior Rate) is responsible for the command to maintain the ship's endurance level (how long it can stay at sea). This is probably our most important task, especially in nuclear submarines, which include the ballistic Trident missile boats 'bombers'. Their main endurance-limiting factor is food (the fuel will last forever). So, I like to think that this essentially means that a chef has control over the UK's nuclear deterrent! Oooh err!

Make no mistake, being a chef anywhere is really hard work, and certain aspects of being in the military can make it even harder. But, when you are next endlessly peeling onions and dreaming of being a sous chef, or listening to the ping of a microwave in a food pub chain, or like I was, just staring at your future with a blank look, remember, you could be enjoying a far more exciting career in the best Navy in the world, whilst spending your down time exploring the world. Just imagine how proud you would be to tell your family and friends what you do for a job. Trust me, if I can do it so can you, just ask my parents.

WO1 Taff Llewellyn MBE

Interested? Visit: www.royalnavy.mod.uk/careers/role-finder and scroll to the catering services branch to find out more or apply. You are under no commitment until after you join HMS Raleigh and sign the Oath of Allegiance.

ROYAL NAVY & ROYAL MARINES CHARITY

Royal Navy chef training: past and present

Naval ships have always required cooks; in the Tudor Navy, a designated cook provided food for the ship's company under the direction of the 'purser'. The term 'purser' (or pusser) is widely used today and predominantly applies to Logistics Officers; catering services, supply chain and administrative personnel answer to them as their Head of Department. Traditionally the cook was recruited from seamen who were significantly aged, of poor physical condition and unable to conduct active duties, usually as a result of a loss of limb(s) – not too dissimilar from today's Warrant Officers Caterers!

In the mid-1800s, the Royal Navy opened its first cookery school in Portsmouth. This was initiated to make cookery more efficient and therefore improve not only the health but the comfort of the crew. The school was such a success that it was decided to open further schools in both Devonport and Chatham in 1902. The course was designed to teach the cooks how to cater for larger numbers of up to 300 men, whilst also being able to understand bakery work. Up until this point, the instructors had all been civilian, but now the level of knowledge and experience was in abundance, the Navy had concluded that it was in a position to train its own staff. Instructors were usually given the rank of Chief Petty Officer.

In 1958 HMS Ceres (the Supply and Secretariat Training School at Wetherby, Yorkshire) moved to Chatham Dockyard as part of HMS Pembroke. At that time, cook training was around 11 weeks long, mirroring the duration of today's Defence Basic Chef Course. The fully trained cook then progressed to a shore establishment for around 9 months to consolidate their training before proceeding to sea.

1983 saw cookery training move to St Omer Barracks, Aldershot, as part of a tri-service cookery school with catering accountancy training undertaken at HMS Raleigh. There will be few still serving that remember the huge tower block with kitchen classrooms over 12 floors, the Navy predominantly occupying floor number 7 with the stipulation that the lift was not to be utilised by trainees; I tried it once, got caught and had to forfeit 7 days' leave!

Cookery training remained at the home of the British Army until 1994 when the Royal Navy Logistics and Supply School launched, enabling both cookery and catering accountancy training to be undertaken at the Defence Maritime Logistics School, HMS Raleigh. It wasn't until 2007 that the first real change in Catering Services structure was initiated; chefs and stewards amalgamated into a single cohort on completion of Senior Rate training to reflect their more managerial role. In 2019, as a reflection of changing attitudes and requirements within the service, the chef and steward branches were combined from initial entry into a single Catering Services Branch. Those legacy chefs and stewards could volunteer to upskill and become Catering Services Ratings; upskilling of both professions fell under Project UNIFY. Training for stewards upskilling to chefs remained at HMS Raleigh until Dec 2021 but the school which had operated in the Plymouth region for the past 25 years finally upped sticks and transferred to Winchester, amalgamating with both Army and RAF cookery schools for the second time. Logistics Branch training is now undertaken at the Defence College of Logistics, Policing and Administration, and whilst the college is headed by an Army Brigadier, the Food Services

Training Wing retains a Cdr RN as its Commanding Officer.

The maritime cohort is headed by an Officer Commanding (Lt Cdr) with one Warrant Officer who, for those that recollect, has had the role of 'travelling assessor' removed from his/her remit. Four Chief Petty Officers undertake Department Co-ordinator, Catering and Policy, Defence Engagement and Front of House and Realistic Working Environment roles; in truth it is these CPOs that keep the many cogs turning and heavily influence the day to day running of the school. Some fourteen instructors, predominantly Petty Officers but with a splattering of Leading Hands, are supported by a number of civil servants to deliver the Defence Basic Chef, Leading Chef, the newly piloted Leading Catering Services and Petty Officer courses, as well as a Senior Rate pre-joining training for those returning to sea in charge roles.

The Defence Basic Chefs course has, at the time of writing, been compressed from eleven to seven weeks intensive training as a result of Covid-19. The construction is so that the craft element of training is undertaken by all three single services and allows for a mix and match of instructors. It would not be unusual to witness a mixed class of Army, RN and RFA students taught by a RAF instructor! The course teaches the fundamentals of pastry and sweet production, some elements of bakery, soup and sauces, cooked meat and fish production, and vegetable and farinaceous dishes, as well as cooking for diversity and catering for vegetarians. Dishes are a far cry from the basic training days of old, and depict dishes more in tune with today's modern style, replicating much of what is taught in industry.

Completion of the Defence Basic course permits students to undertake a 'Bravo Phase' – this essentially marinizes the individual and prepares him or her for life at sea. The Royal Navy is fortunate to have at its disposal a purpose-built Realistic Working Environment (RWE); constructed in 2019 it superbly imitates a Type 45 Galley and immerses individuals into watch routines, allows introduction to due diligence recording, health and safety, and, importantly, instils teamwork. For those that recollect the part IV training at the numerous Shore Establishments, the RWE attempts to go some way to mirror this.

Leading Chef/Leading Catering Services courses allow seven of the allocated nineteen weeks devoted to advanced cookery. My most senior and experienced Leading Hand Instructor, Mattie Tew, who incidentally is the brains behind this publication, has devoted significant time and effort into developing a course which encompasses modern day cookery techniques. Whilst some methods remain from the bygone years and a number of dishes thought to be generated from the 60s and 70s, such as Hasselback potatoes, oxtail au von and lobster thermidor, begin to make a revamped reappearance, gone are the socles and dishes awash with aspic, replaced with some fine dining fare that would grace any top restaurant.

WO1(CS) Tony Shelley – Logistics Training Officer, Food Services Training Wing (Maritime)

The Royal Navy Culinary Arts Team: past, present and future

Kidney bean glazers, jam queens, stove-top ballerinas or prima donnas… call us what you like, one thing is for certain: the Royal Navy Culinary Arts Team (RNCAT) has been a long-standing feature of the Royal Navy Chef's branch for a lot longer than people know or think. As the current team captain, it is my privilege to give a brief history of the Royal Navy Culinary Arts Team and to explain the team's involvement in the wider industry competition circuit and the Combined Services Culinary Arts Team (CSCAT).

There is no actual confirmed date or evidence to document when the Royal Navy Culinary Arts Team was first established. However, having picked the brains of legendary champions within past teams, there was a small group of chefs who competed as far back as 1960. This pioneering group would travel the country entering many prestigious shows such as Hotelympia, which back then was held annually at Olympia in London and still takes place today (albeit biannually and in the ExCell Centre). Back in the day, the competition circuit was rigid and all dishes had to go through a strict inspection process to ensure they were 'fit for display'. In fact receiving a certificate of acceptance was an achievement in itself, and was something to be extremely proud of – this process of elimination remained right up to the late 1980s, when the procedure was changed to what we know today.

I spoke to the illustrious past team captain Mr Nick Vardis for a brief précis of his time in and around the team. He fondly recalls his initial chef training in 1974 at the Royal Navy Cookery School, HMS Pembroke in Chatham, gazing in amazement into a display cabinet in the main foyer and seeing numerous trophies and large gold medals, then actually meeting the legendary

Fleet Chief Chef (Warrant Officer) of the school, Mr Ken Frazer, the chef who had won all the medals and trophies on display in the foyer. This was where he realised that there was a serious bunch of instructors who competed regularly and won many amazing medals and trophies. This was to become Nick's driving force, as he put it, and it ignited the fire in him to want to be part of this special team and to compete on the national and international stage. He went on to do this, representing the RNCAT and CSCAT, and ultimately becoming the England Culinary Arts Team Captain.

The True RNCAT opened to be a more inclusive team in the late 70s early 80s, which enabled them to have grater reach and more numbers to compete. By the middle of the 80s there was a regular team of RN chefs who would compete nationally from North to South, and London to Torquay. It was in the late 80s that the first Royal Navy Salon Culinaire was held in HMS Nelson, Portsmouth. This was well attended, but initially only involved display dishes, such as cakes, platters and plates. It was a few years later that the live cookery elements of the competition began, with purpose-built competition kitchens being introduced.

Sadly at the time but fortunately enough for the present day, as the years went by and the three services numbers decreased, the decision was made to combine energies to create a tri-service event and the Combined Services Culinary Arts Competition was born, which still takes place today albeit under a different name. Initially taking place in Portsmouth and Aldershot, as time progressed it was opened to the wider services. Today it is known as Exercise Joint Caterer, and combines both the front of house and cooking in various classes, and has even had a tenure at Sandown Park Racecourse

and the Defence Academy at MOD Shrivenham. The advantage of a combined event is that it assists in identifying the cream of the crop from all three services to form the Combined Services Culinary Arts Team (CSCAT). Their first ever competitive run out was in 1996 at Hotelympia, where they won gold for the team event and then went on to compete on the world stage in the Culinary World Cup and the Culinary Olympics. This practice continues today with the CSCAT being equally split with 12 members of each service combining to form the current squad.

My first personal experience or involvement with the culinary arts events was way back in 1997. When I was assigned to HMS Nelson Senior Rates Mess, my WOCA at the time (WOCA Trevor Quickfall) informed me that I was taking part in the Tri Services Junior Chef of the Year. Luckily for me, after a short time to practice and some excellent guidance and mentoring, I won! I received a gold medal, Best in Class plate and, of course, the title Tri Services Junior Chef of the Year. I was then consequently selected to compete for the

combined team at Hotelympia in 1998 and won silver and bronze medals in separate events, of which I am extremely proud.

Since then I have gone on to compete for the RNCAT in the USA twice and, as I have already said, I am the current RNCAT captain, a position I cherish and feel honoured to hold. Although my competing days are now over, I am fortunate to be still heavily involved with the mentoring and growth of the future superstars within the Catering Services branch, something I wish to do till I hang up my apron for good.

So, if you think us kidney bean glazers are all full of self-importance and we act as if we are the bee's knees when turning and burning in the galley, then that's fine by me… and it's probably because we are.

'Don't knock till you have tried it' is my philosophy. Thank you for letting me reminisce and spin a dit.

WO2 Si 'Little-Chef' Geldart
RNCAT Team Captain

Arthur William Hayne

Arthur William Hayne was born in 1905, volunteered for service in 1923 and retired in 1945. His handwritten cookery book was donated by his daughter, Julie Wallace, to be shared in this book along with her father's story and his enduring love of the Royal Navy.

A chance conversation with Julie's friend, Rear Admiral Terry Loughran, led to her father's old recipe collection being unearthed in a drawer and presented to the cookery school at HMS Raleigh. By coincidence, Arthur had spent two years working in the wardroom there, where his handwritten book was brought back into use. Thanks to Admiral Loughran's insistence that this piece of family and naval history should be showcased, Julie was able to visit the cookery school for a tour, a lunch and, most importantly, to meet the people who were planning to produce a cookbook in support of the Royal Navy and Royal Marines Charity.

Julie describes her father as a Navy man through and through, who was dedicated to the service despite his career being cut short by retirement due to ill health. In a way though, Arthur never left the Navy, even after his 22 years of service, because he found a job at the local naval air station, HMS Heron near Yeovil. He worked there until his retirement in 1965 at the age of 70, having had various duties including updating the naval records, which involved meeting a courier from the London train every week, with whom he would exchange a briefcase that contained the latest amendments to the records.

Arthur loved being in the Navy and it shaped his whole life, beginning with his determination to join up as a young man. He was from a farming family, but he neither wanted to follow his father's and older brother's path, nor find work at the gloving factory in the village. Instead,

Arthur took lessons with a doctor who lived nearby and studied in order to pass the exams that would enable him to go straight into Petty Officer training. His naval career began in the kitchen; he was initially a chef and it was during that time that he wrote up the many original recipes he learnt to cook in the Navy. The book was passed down and kept by Julie, who wanted some way of immortalising such a unique piece of her father's past.

Although the heat of the galley wasn't for him, Arthur went on to become a captain's steward, a role which Julie credits for how good he was with people. He was someone who wanted to do things with purpose and to a high standard, but also a thoughtful man who would bring back unusual gifts for his children, always on the lookout for something special and a little different. He enjoyed being stationed in South Africa and grew to love the country that introduced him to the 'avocado pear', which he was very keen on, though it wasn't easy to find back home at the time! Visiting these far-flung places had some downsides, including malaria, which he suffered multiple times and eventually caused him to be invalided from the Navy. However, it also saved his life when he was taken off a ship due to his ill health, not long before it was blown up by a mine in the Mediterranean.

Many more stories about Arthur's time in the Navy have been passed down through Julie's family, and she still lives in one of the cottages formerly owned by his family near their farms. He knew that a quiet agricultural life was not for him though, and was determined to try his best and to better himself every day. Julie of course remembers him with great affection, and is delighted to have his past brought to light and credit given to his service in the Royal Navy, which always meant so much to him.

Royal Navy traditional dinners and events

The Royal Navy chefs provide up to four meals a day, 365 days of the year, in all four corners of the world – at sea, under the sea and ashore. There are also occasions when they are able to show off their skills, providing the food at grand occasions, some of which boast a history and traditions stretching back over 200 years.

Trafalgar Night Dinner

The Battle of Trafalgar saw Britain secure victory over the French and Spanish fleet off Cape Trafalgar, giving the Royal Navy its most famous triumph. The battle also immortalised the memory of Lord Vice-Admiral Horatio Nelson, who, with 27 ships-of-the-line, inflicted defeat on a numerically superior Franco-Spanish fleet. Nelson was hit by a musket ball on the Redoutable and died on HMS Victory's Orlop Deck.

Trafalgar Day is the most important day in the calendar of HMS Victory, the oldest commissioned warship in the world. Britain's wealth, prosperity and status as a nation on the world stage still owe much to the courage and skill of the crews of the British ships and their great leader, Admiral Lord Nelson, that momentous day off Cape Trafalgar.

Every year, commissioned officers of the Royal Navy commemorate the victory and passing of Lord Vice-Admiral Nelson by holding a Trafalgar Night dinner in the Officers' Mess.

This commemorative dinner is a grand affair including the 'Parading of the Beef' and chocolate ships known as 'Ships of the Line'. It is held on, or close to, the 21st October to coincide with the battle on the same date in 1805. Other interested parties across the world also hold Trafalgar Night dinners in commemoration of the battle and Lord Nelson.

There is no fixed menu for this occasion, but it would usually consist of at least a fish course/starter, beef main course and a sweet all named with a Nelson/Trafalgar twist. This would be followed by coffee and mints, as well as passing of the Port (to the left).

The Loyal Toast: Diners should stand – the Loyal Toast is traditionally given to toast the reigning monarch. For naval officers it is customary to remain seated during the Loyal Toast. The tradition dates back to Tudor times when standing up to drink a toast onboard a ship-of-the-line invariably meant bumping your head on the low beams. Charles II is reported to have said, "I'll see that my naval officers run no such risk, for I will allow them from henceforth to remain sitting when drinking my health".

The Immortal Memory Toast: A Trafalgar Night speech is usually made by a guest of honour. The proposer of the toast will precede it with some Nelsonian comments, which can vary in length. The toast itself is 'the Immortal Memory' and is drunk standing in total silence. This is customary out of respect of the memory of the Admiral.

For the 200th anniversary, the original toast was reinstated and used by HM The Queen, which is as follows:

"The Immortal Memory of Lord Nelson and those who fell with him."

Pickle Night

In contrast to the grand affair of the Trafalgar Night Dinner in the Wardroom, Pickle Night is a less formal event held in the Warrant Officers and Senior Rates mess, although it does come with its traditional format, and fines will be handed out for those not abiding by the rules. Although linked to the events of the battle of Trafalgar the Pickle Night is a relatively new event, and was the brainchild of then Commodore of the Royal Naval Barracks in Portsmouth, Commodore Lea, and the President of the Warrant Officers and Chief Petty Officers' Mess, Warrant Officer Hetherington, in 1974.

Pickle Night celebrates the arrival of HMS Pickle in England, carrying the news of the Battle of Trafalgar. Participants wear 1805 sailor or marine dress complete with straw hat and stripy jumpers. There is no set menu but everything is traditionally eaten from the same bowl, using the same spoon and drinking from the same pot/glass. Should you lose any of these items during the evening, you can expect more fines.

The Pickle Night format varies according to its ship, establishment or civilian setting, but the basics for all good organisers are as follows:

Pickle Night

Serial	Time	Action	Remarks
1	1930	Arrival of Ship's Company	Mess for pre-drinks
2	1955	Dinner Call All Shipmates not dining at the Captain's table are to follow the COXN and take their place behind their seats	President and top table to follow on after guests
3	2000	President will bring down gavel once Evening rules	Master At Arms to present the evening rules
4	2005	Grog dit/Grog issue	Grog
5	o/c	Grace	Master At Arms
6	2010	First Course	Mess cooks collect & serve
7	o/c	President will bring down gavel once and first despatch will be read	Gun Commander
8	o/c	After short pause, President will bring down gavel once and second despatch will be read	Gun Commander
9	2030	One all round	
10	o/c	Main course	Mess cooks collect & serve
11	o/c	President will bring down gavel once and third despatch will be read	Gun Commander
12	o/c	After short pause, President will bring down gavel once and fouth despatch will be read	Gun Commander
13	2055	Pudding	Mess cooks collect & serve
14	o/c	President will bring down gavel once and fifth despatch will be read	Gun Commander
15	o/c	After short pause, President will bring down gavel once and sixth despatch will be read	Gun Commander
16	o/c	One all round	10 mins
17	o/c	Place settings cleared, issue Port to Gun Commanders	
18	o/c	The President and Gun Commanders slide the bottle to the person on their left. That person pours a tot, and so on. The last person to receive the bottle will be the President and Gun Commanders	
19	o/c	Seventh despatch	
20	o/c	The President will bring down the gavel once, toast Nelson. This is the only toast in the Royal Navy that is drunk in SILENCE. No response to be given	Nelson's Toast: "The Immortal Memory of Lord Nelson and those who fell with him"
21		Eighth despatch	
22	o/c	The President will bring down gavel four times: "Master At Arms, do you have any white rats?"	Master At Arms will respond
23	o/c	Commanders table	
24	o/c	President speech	
25	o/c	Loyal Toast "The Queen"	All remain seated
26	o/c	All will move from tables for making merriment	

Pickle Night: The Despatches

Despatch 1

To be read on completion of the First Course by:

Insert name, Gun #

Captain Sir, Distinguished Guests, shipmates

The date is the 1st October 1805, the place, 50 miles off Cadiz and His Majesty's schooner PICKLE has covered a distance of approximately 1000 miles from Plymouth in 8 days to join up with the Battle Fleet of Admiral Nelson.

Three days later Nelson Despatches PICKLE to help EURYALUS and HYDRA to keep vigil on the combined French and Spanish Fleets in Cadiz harbour.

Despatch 2

To be read following a short pause after Despatch 1 by:

Insert name, Gun #

The date is 20th October 1805 and the enemy fleet has set sail from Cadiz and set course for the Straits of Gibraltar to seek out the English Fleet.

Despatch 3

To be read on completion of the Main Course by:

Insert name, Gun #

The date is 21st of October 1805, the place Cape Trafalgar and the opposing Fleets meet in battle. During the battle PICKLE is engaged in picking up survivors and prisoners as ordered. One of the prisoners is a young Frenchwoman who was rescued from the water by a boat from PICKLE.

She was the wife of a sailor from the French ship ACHILLE which caught fire and blew up. She escaped by climbing out onto the rudder where she was burned by molten lead dripping onto her neck and shoulders then jumping into the water. Her burns were treated by the sailors of

PICKLE; she was given seaman's clothing and transferred to REVENGE for transportation back to England.

Despatch 4

To be read following a short pause after Despatch 3 by:

Insert name, Gun #

The battle over, the British Fleet has won a decisive victory over the enemy, but, alas, Nelson has been mortally wounded. Admiral Collingwood has taken command of the Fleet and shifted his flag from ROYAL SOVEREIGN to EURYALUS.

Admiral Collingwood decides to send his Despatches back to England with the news of the Glorious Victory and the death of our most famous Admiral.

He chooses the second smallest ship PICKLE commanded by Lt John Richards Lapenotiere, a personal favourite of his as a result of an incident some years previously, when they were travelling together as passengers on a ship. On that occasion, the helmsman was given the order, which, if carried out, would have resulted in the vessel running aground. Lapenotiere seeing the danger took over command and saved the ship.

Despatch 5

To be read after the Sweet Course by:

Insert name, Gun #

The date is the 26th of October 1805 and PICKLE heads for England with a crew of thirty-two: 17 English, 1 Scot, 9 Irish, 1 Welshman, 1 Norwegian and a Channel Islander.

The journey was both eventful and hazardous, with gales, during which she was holed and flooded. This was followed by a lack of wind when her crew rowed her to keep her on course at a steady speed of two knots.

Despatch 6

To be read following a short pause after Despatch 5 by:

Insert name, Gun #

The date is now the 4th of November 1805, the place Falmouth and PICKLE has covered the distance once again in eight days.

In Falmouth Bay she drops anchor and the jollyboat conveys Lapenotiere ashore where a post-chaise is waiting to take him to London, a distance of 271 miles. Lapenotiere will change horses 21 times on the journey. Astoundingly they cover the distance in 37 hours, arriving at 0100, Wednesday the 6th of November with Collingwood's Despatches, dated the 22nd of October 1805 and addressed to one William Marsden, Secretary to the Board of the Admiralty.

The First Sea Lord, Lord Barham, was roused from his bed to peruse them and they continued at business until 0500 when a messenger was sent off to His Majesty King George III at Windsor.

Despatch 7

To be read after tables are cleared by:

Insert name, Gun #

Captain Sir, Distinguished Guests, shipmates

The following appeared in The Times dated Thursday the 7th of November 1805:

"The ever to be lamented death of Lord Viscount Nelson, Duke of Bronte, The Commander in Chief who fell in the action of the 21st in the Arms of Victory, covered with Glory, whose memory will ever be dear to the British Navy and the British Nations, whose zeal for the honour of his King and for the interests of his country will ever be held up as a shining example for the British Seaman – Leaves to me a duty to return my thanks, to the Right Honourable Rear Admiral, Captains, Offices, Seamen and detachment of Royal Marines serving on board His Majesty's Squadron now under my command for the conduct on that day."

Despatch 8 Final Despatch

To be read after The Immortal Memory:

Insert name, Gun #

"But where can I find language to express my sentiments of the valour and skill which were displayed by the Officers, the Seamen and Marines in the battle with the enemy, where every individual appeared a hero on whom the Glory of His Country depended?

The attack was irresistible and the issue of it adds to the Pages of Naval Annals a brilliant instance of what Britons can do when their King and their Country need their Service.

To the Right Honourable Rear Admiral, The Earl of Northesk, to the Captains, Officers, and Seamen and to the Officers, Non-Commissioned Officers and Privates of the Royal Marines, I beg to give my sincere and hearty thanks for their highly and meritorious conduct, both in the action and in their zeal and activity in bringing the captured ships out from the perilous situation in which they were after their surrender, among the Shoals of Trafalgar, in boisterous weather.

And I desire that the respective Captains will be pleased to communicate to the Officers, Seamen and Royal Marines this testimony of my high approbation of their conduct and my thanks for it."

Taranto Night

Taranto Night is the Fleet Air Arm's annual celebration of the Battle of Taranto on the night of 11 November 1940. Taranto, a coastal city in the 'heel' of southern Italy, was home port to the Italian Grand Fleet, which posed a considerable threat to allied operations in the Mediterranean. It was determined that an attack on the Italian battleships in the heavily defended harbour was required, to be called Operation Judgment. 21 elderly, open-cockpit Swordfish biplane aircraft launched in darkness from HMS Illustrious, late in the evening of 11 November. In radio silence and with only a compass to guide them, flying over 170 miles in two waves, the aircraft carried out bombing and torpedo attacks under extremely heavy, close-quarters enemy fire before returning to the carrier. The damage inflicted on the Italian fleet effectively removed it from the war – over half the fleet was sunk or damaged beyond repair. Two Swordfish were shot down. The crew of two from the first were taken prisoner; the crew of the second were killed.

After the successful attack, Admiral Cunningham noted: "Taranto, and the night of 11–12 November 1940, should be remembered forever as having shown once and for all that in the Fleet Air Arm the Navy has its most devastating weapon." Dedicated to the 'Men of Taranto' and celebrated around the world in Her Majesty's Ships and Royal Naval Air Stations, the evening is a formal Naval Mess Dinner, but with a twist. Tradition dictates that junior aircrew stage a re-enactment of the battle, often with several scenes interspersed between courses of the dinner. The 'Skit' – an historical vignette of the Battle of Taranto – is the highlight of the evening. Winston Churchill described Taranto as a 'Glorious Episode' and in recognition the original concept was a short, humorous sketch, which involved model Swordfish aircraft descending on wires suspended from the dining room ceiling, diving to attack cardboard cut-out ships accompanied by loud thunder flashes, anti-aircraft fire and copious amounts of smoke.

Over the years, the skit has developed into a truly Oscar-worthy event! Where safety permits, the use of pyrotechnics to simulate the attacks is positively encouraged – the more impressive the better! In more modern times, extensive use has been made of video sketches combined with live acting, often making jovial comparisons to contemporary events. The 'Players' will represent their Italian counterparts, complete with accents and Italian costumes, as well as the brave Men of Taranto themselves. It serves as an inspiring reminder of the indomitable spirit of the Fleet Air Arm epitomised by a small band of young naval aviators in 1940.

The added dimension of the re-enactment often makes Taranto Night one of the most popular in a Ship's or Establishment's social calendar. When everyone is seated, the single bang of the President's gavel for Grace signals that dinner has officially begun. There is no set menu, but a nod to Italian cuisine can be expected in one of the courses, and a fish course of swordfish steaks is often included. The President and Guest Speaker traditionally give rousing speeches about the historical significance of Taranto which are accompanied by banging of tables in agreement.

Rules of Order apply throughout the dinner and misbehaviour or breaking them results in disciplinary action. The President can order the culprit to leave the Mess, fine him a number of drinks or give him a chance to exonerate himself by the use of his wits. Fines vary from a single drink to drinks for all present. It's renowned for high jinks, with Officers' Mess bills taking a hammering!

Passing the Port is an important naval tradition. When the last course has finished and the tables cleared, the President bangs the gavel for silence and calls for the second Grace. The Port is always passed to the left. Unlike Pickle night, Port decanters are passed by sliding them along the table and they are lifted only to pour. In common with all Naval Mess Dinners, Royal Navy Officers are permitted to remain seated for the Loyal Toast, traditionally given to toast the reigning monarch.

Burns Night Supper/Dinner

Although not a naval-themed event, the life of Scottish poet Robert Burns is celebrated in all wardrooms by naval officers. The evening is normally a formal event and unlike most other dinners does have a more traditional menu, although this can be changed as required:

Starter: Cock a Leekie Soup

Main course: Haggis with Neeps and Tatties (turnips and mashed potato)

Dessert: Clootie Dumpling or Cranachan (a traditional dessert of oats, cream, whisky and raspberries)

Drink: Scotch whisky

A traditional Burns Night Supper/Dinner in a wardroom would also follow the traditional format as a similar event 'ashore':

Piping in the guests – to bagpipe or traditional music

Reciting of the Selkirk Grace

Piping in the haggis – guests stand to welcome the haggis to the table!

Toast to the haggis – honouring the most important ingredient of the meal

Burns Night meal

The Immortal Memory – an account of the life of Robbie Burns, followed by Burns' songs and poems

Toast to the Lassies – a traditional thank you to the women involved in the preparations (and a light-hearted homage to Burns' love of women)

Finale with Auld Lang Syne

The Selkirk Grace is recited after the guests have entered the room and are seated at the table and before the haggis is piped to the table:

"Some hae meat and canna eat,

And some wad eat that want it,

But we hae meat and we can eat,

And sae the Lord be thankit."

The **Immortal Memory** is the centrepiece of the evening and equivalent to a wedding dinner speech. The denoted speaker gives a talk on the life of Robert Burns, in anticipation of the songs and poems to come. Although the speech often touches on the highs and lows of Burns' life, it should include a celebration of his home country of Scotland, his literary genius and his love of all things Scottish.

Toasts

The Royal Navy has a tradition of daily toasts normally proposed by the youngest present. In June 2013 the Tuesday and Saturday toasts were officially changed under orders from the Second Sea Lord, Vice-Admiral David Steel, to reflect the fact that women have been at sea in the Royal Navy for nearly two decades.

Sunday: *"Absent friends"*

Monday: *"Our ships at sea"*

Tuesday: *"Our sailors" (prior to 2013, "Our men")*

Wednesday: *"Ourselves" (usually with the informal reply "for nobody else will concern themselves with our well-being!")*

Thursday: *"A bloody war or a sickly season"*

Friday: *"A willing foe and sea-room"*

Saturday: *"Our families" (prior to 2013, "Our wives and sweethearts," usually with the reply "May they never meet!")*

Balls

The Officers' and Senior Rates' messes will normally host two Balls a year, one in the summer and one at Christmas or Winter, which are often themed events decided by the mess committee. Unlike the traditional dinners, they do not generally follow a particular format. A Ball is another occasion when the Royal Navy Catering Services teams get to show what they can really do. The food at a Christmas/Winter Ball would ordinarily be a carvery-style occasion prepared to the highest standard. The evening would also include various forms of entertainment culminating in 'carriages' provided at the end of the night/morning.

The Summer Ball is probably the largest, most lavish event in the diary, for which the chef is provided the largest budget of the year with the expectation to provide the wow factor. The simplest way to describe the food at a Summer Ball would be to call it a cold buffet. That description though, would be a disservice. The days of dressed salmon and chaud froid hams of the 70s and 80s have passed to be replaced with competition-standard platters using the best ingredients and modern techniques. As with the Christmas/Winter Ball, the evening would be full of entertainment, anything from a casino to a full-on fairground, finishing with 'carriages' at the end of the event.

Defence Engagement

Defence Engagement is about influence and is an important occasion whenever a ship makes a port visit, usually held on the evening of arrival. Traditionally known as a 'Cocktail Party', this modern version normally involves most of a Ships Company hosting local dignitaries or putting on displays around the ship. The refreshments for the evening will be a variety canapes, petits fours and cold drinks (alcohol dependant on location). The evening will finish with Ceremonial Sunset, followed by guests departing and leave being granted.

Bob Field
Fundraising and Merchandise Manager RNRMC
WO1 CS (Rtd)

RECIPES & CHEFS

The official diet of the Royal Navy

Here are some sample recipes to give you a taste of the traditional Navy diet from a time when Vice-Admiral Horatio Nelson ruled the waves...

The official diet consisted of the following:

Sunday: 1lb. biscuit, 1lb. salt pork, ½ pint peas	**Monday:** 1lb. biscuit, 1 pint oatmeal, 2oz. butter
Tuesday: 1lb. biscuit, 2lbs. salt beef	**Wednesday:** 1lb. biscuit, ½ pint peas, 1 pint oatmeal, 2oz. butter, 4oz. cheese
Thursday: Same as Sunday	**Friday:** Same as Monday
Saturday: Same as Tuesday	

Sample a sailor's diet

Remember, the following recipes are a full sailor's portion – if only sampling the dishes, make a proportionate amount to avoid waste:

Hard Tack or Ship's Biscuit

2 cups plain flour

½ tsp salt

½-¾ cups water

Mix the flour and salt together, then add enough water to make a very stiff dough. Knead the dough for a few minutes, then beat with a rolling pin until flat, about 1cm thick. Cut into 5cm x 5cm sections. With a fork, punch it full of holes. Bake in an ungreased, flat pan at 250°f (125°c) for 2-3 hours.

Peas and Salt Pork

1lb. salt pork

½ pint dried peas

¾ quarts water

Salt and pepper

Soak the pork and peas separately in cold water overnight. Cut the pork into bite-size pieces and place in a pot with the peas, along with the water. Bring to the boil, then reduce heat and simmer until the peas have turned to mush. Salt and pepper to taste.

Burgoo (Oatmeal)

½ pint steel-cut oats

2 cups water

1½-2 tbsp butter

2 tsp sugar

Salt

Gradually add the water to the oats. Bring to a boil over a medium heat, then reduce the heat and simmer until the oats are tender. Transfer to bowls and add butter, sugar and salt to taste, stirring until dissolved.

Pudding

In place of meat, a sailor might have been given 'pudding:'

¼lb. suet

2lbs. plain flour

½lb. raisins or ¼lb. dried currants

Approx. 2 cups water

Mince or grate the suet after removing all meat and connective tissues. Mix into the flour thoroughly, then add enough water to make a stiff dough. A little sugar can be added if desired. Add the raisins or currants and mix again to distribute them evenly throughout the pudding. Dampen a large cotton cloth, wringing out the excess water very well. Flour the centre and place the pudding in the centre of the cloth. Pull up the edges and, making sure that all the edges are gathered into the centre, tie a cotton string around the 'neck' of the package. Lower into boiling water and, making sure it is completely covered, boil for about 1½ hours.

Leftover pudding can be sliced and fried in butter.

Going ashore, a sailor would have eaten the same foods as others of his class. Their diet may have included some of the following popular items.

Baked Beans

2lbs. white pea (navy) beans

1 tbsp salt

¾lb. salt pork

½ cup maple sugar (or syrup) or brown sugar or molasses

Soak the beans overnight in a pot covered by twice the volume of water. In the morning, change the water (drain and add new). Add the salt, bring to a boil, then simmer until tender. Slice the salt pork and put into the pot with the beans. Add the maple sugar and put on a tight lid. If you like, you can add ½ tsp dry mustard, some chopped onion, or an onion studded with cloves. Bake at 250°f (125°c) for 8-10 hours.

Corned Beef and Cabbage

4lbs. corned beef brisket

1 tsp thyme

1 onion stuck with cloves

3 onions

6 carrots

2lbs. cabbages

Pepper

Fill a large pot with cold water. Add the beef and spices. Bring to the boil. Add the onions and carrots and return to the boil. Then simmer gently for 3 hours. Remove the cloved onion. Quarter the cabbages, add to pot and simmer half an hour – until cabbage is tender. Drain and serve, dotted with butter and well peppered. Boiled potatoes were often eaten with this.

Bramble Dunfillan

¼ cup butter

1 cup plain flour

¾ cup sugar

1 egg

2 tbsp milk

¼ tsp baking powder

1 tsp grated lemon rind

1lb. fresh brambles (blackberries)

Cut the butter into the flour until crumbly, then mix in ¼ cup of the sugar. Beat the egg and combine with the milk and baking powder. Blend with the flour thoroughly. Mix in the grated lemon rind. Stew the berries with the remaining ½ cup of sugar and water to cover. When the berries are tender, spoon the batter over them. Bake for 20 minutes at 350°f (175°c).

Michel Roux Jr's
Gigot d'Agneau de Sept Heures

Translated as Leg of Lamb Cooked for Seven Hours, this rich dish contains two and a half bottles of red wine and half a bottle of Port! The lamb is marinated a week in advance. This lengthy marinating time, along with the slow cooking process, renders it incredibly tender and flavoursome.

Preparation time: 1 hour, plus 8 days | Cooking time: 7 hours | Serves 8

Ingredients

3kg leg of lamb
200g pork back fat
100g unsalted butter
2 tbsp olive oil
1 onion & 1 carrot, sliced
1 celery stick, chopped
150g smoked bacon
2 bottles of full-bodied red wine
½ bottle of Port
3 litres veal stock
Salt and pepper

For the marinade

½ bottle of full-bodied red wine
2 cloves of garlic, crushed
1 small onion, thickly sliced
1 sprig of each thyme
& rosemary
2 tbsp extra-virgin olive oil
2 cloves
1 tbsp white peppercorns
3 tbsp brandy
2 tbsp red wine vinegar

Method

Trim the lamb, remove the aitch bone and lightly score the skin. Your butcher will do this for you.

Cut 12cm long strips of pork back fat and use these to lard the lamb lengthways at least 6 times with a knife or a larding needle.

Mix all the marinade ingredients together, add the lamb and cover with cling film. Place in the fridge and leave to marinate for a week, turning the meat several times a day so it absorbs the flavours.

Drain the lamb, reserving the liquid and the onion. Heat the butter and oil in a thick-based braising pan, add the lamb and cook over medium-high heat until golden brown. Remove the lamb from the pan and, if the fat is burned, discard the fat and use fresh butter to cook all the vegetables (including the marinade onion) until golden brown.

Add the bacon, then deglaze the pan with the wine, Port and reserved marinade.

Place the pan over high heat and reduce the liquid by two-thirds, then add the lamb, season well and cover with the veal stock. Bring to the boil and skim.

Check the seasoning. Put a lid on the pan and place it in the oven at 140°c for approximately 7 hours. (Keep an eye on it, though as ovens vary and you may have to top up the liquid with some water occasionally. Also, the cooking time may vary depending on the age and quality of the lamb. The meat should be tender and nearly falling off the bone.)

Take the lamb out of the oven and leave it to cool in the sauce. When the lamb is cold, remove it from the pan and strain the sauce through a fine sieve. Check for seasoning and consistency; reduce the sauce if necessary.

Pour the sauce over the meat and leave it in the fridge overnight.

The next day, when you are ready to serve, reheat the meat gently in the sauce in a pan on the hob, while basting occasionally. Bring it to the table and serve with a spoon – don't attempt to carve. This is good served with mashed potatoes.

RECIPES
& CHEFS
CALUM
RICHARDSON

Calum Richardson

Chef/Director of world-famous The Bay Fish and Chips, Calum Richardson is well known for his passion for sustainability and the environment.

"The Royal Navy has been a big part of my life, and it helped me to build the life skills that you would not learn anywhere else. I joined the Royal Navy in 1989 at the age of 16. In the next 10 years, my career took me on ships like HMS Liverpool and HMS Sandown. It wasn't the career I had planned, and instead of becoming a chef, I was assigned as a Marine Engineering Mechanic. However, this role developed me in so many ways – it gave me the skills needed to become a successful business owner and helped me gain confidence working on my own, but also being a team member and trusting the people around me.

Not long after leaving the Royal Navy, I began working in a fish and chip business and I was proud to win UK's Young Fish Fryer of the Year for 2002-2004. Here began my career in the hospitality industry – and I haven't looked back.

I opened The Bay Fish and Chips in 2006 and it has since become one of the UK's highest-rated fish and chip shops. We were named the UK's No.1 independent takeaway at The National Fish and Chip Awards in 2013, an award which is one of over 60 accolades we have accumulated so far.

The Bay Fish and Chips is one of the Compass Group suppliers and we are proud to be serving The Bay's batter and fishcakes to Royal Navy bases, as well as UK airports, sports stadiums, schools and hospitals around the country.

My time within the Royal Navy and spending a big part of my life at sea has changed my view on how we treat nature, and thus impacted how I run my business. The Bay is one of the most sustainable fish and chips shops in the world, and I was honoured to make the list as Britain's highest-ranking entry in The Lonely Planet Eating Guide, placing at number 31. Sustainability is at the heart of the business at The Bay.

I started a business consultancy with the aim of helping to develop and mentor young people, something which has always been a big passion of mine. I am closely involved with training young chefs within the National Federation of Fish Friers, and I enjoy seeing them achieve their full potential and uphold the highest standards."

The Bay Smoked Haddock Scotch Egg
with Garlic Aioli

I love the flavour of smoked haddock and if you are not a big fish-lover, this is a great way to introduce it into your diet. This dish allows you to use small, broken pieces of fish which can be picked up from the local fishmonger. An easy dish to be prepared earlier in the day and finished off just before service.

Preparation time: 35 minutes | Cooking time: 5 minutes | Serves 4

Ingredients

For the Scotch eggs

170g floury potatoes, peeled and quartered

15ml rapeseed oil

200g smoked haddock, cubed

Few dashes white wine vinegar

4 quail's eggs

1 egg, beaten & 50g flour

75g bread or panko crumbs

Vegetable oil, for frying

For the herb oil

100g mixed soft herbs (basil, dill, parsley, chives and chervil)

200ml rapeseed oil

For the aioli

1 slice of stale bread, soaked in water

1 clove of garlic

1 lemon, zested and juiced

100ml rapeseed oil

Salt and pepper

For the salad

75g mixed leaves

55g fennel, finely shredded

20g tomato, diced

16 small pickled onions

4 pickled beetroots, quartered

Salt and pepper

Method

For the Scotch eggs

Cook the potatoes in salted boiling water for 15-20 minutes until tender. Drain and mash. Place a pan over a very low heat and add the oil. Add the smoked fish and cook for 4 minutes, stirring so that it cooks evenly. Flake the fish with the back of a fork. Add the mashed potato to the pan and mix until a thick paste is formed. Set aside to cool. Prepare a bowl of iced water and the white wine vinegar. Bring a large pan of water to the boil, lower in the quail's eggs, cook for exactly 3 minutes, then place into the iced water. Once cool, peel immediately. Take one quarter of the fish mixture in the palm of your hand, make a dent in the centre and place a quail's egg in the dent. Close your hand over the egg so that you cover it with the rest of the mixture. Roll the coated egg in your hands to make sure it is evenly covered. Repeat for each egg, then place on a plate lined with cling film and put in the fridge for 1 hour. Take three shallow bowls and put the egg in one, the flour in another and the breadcrumbs in the other. Dip each Scotch egg into the flour, then the egg, then the breadcrumbs, ensuring they are well coated.

For the herb oil

Prepare a bowl of iced water and bring a large pan of lightly salted water to the boil. Blanch the soft herbs for 30 seconds, then transfer to the iced water. Leave for 5 minutes to go cold. Squeeze the excess water from the herbs and drain on a cloth. Place the drained herbs into a blender with a little rapeseed oil. Blend to a thick purée, then add the remaining oil. Keep blending for 5 minutes until the sides feel slightly warm. Strain the purée through a double layer of clean muslin into a bowl; leave for 10 minutes to ensure the green oil has passed through. Place in the fridge.

For the aioli

Place the bread into a food processor with the garlic, lemon zest and juice. Blend while gradually adding the rapeseed oil. Season to taste. Place in the fridge.

To serve

Preheat the oil to 175°c in a deep fryer. Fry the Scotch eggs for 2 minutes or until golden brown. Drain on kitchen paper. Mix the salad except the shredded fennel. Dress with the herb oil then plate. Take a spoonful of the aioli and place to the side of the salad, then put a little fennel on top. Halve the Scotch egg and place on top.

Pan-roasted Cod Loin with Arbroath Smokie Risotto and Herb Oil

Cod is under-used in Scotland, but a fantastic fish that does not take much preparation or cooking. Arbroath Smokie is unique to this area and has a wonderful natural flavour that ties in perfectly with a risotto. Arbroath Smokie brings back childhood memories of being with my dad. This is my 'go to' dish on a 'driech' (wet and miserable) day.

Preparation time: 20 minutes | Cooking time: 50 minutes | Serves 4

Ingredients

For the Arbroath smokie
200ml milk
200g Arbroath smokie

For the herb oil
100g mixed soft herbs (basil, dill, parsley, chives and chervil)
200ml rapeseed oil

For the risotto
30g butter
20g shallot, finely diced
50g small leek, finely diced
1 clove of garlic, crushed
1 sprig of thyme
100ml white wine
200g risotto rice
500ml fish stock
15g crème fraîche
Salt and pepper

For the cod
4 x 175g cod loin
Rapeseed oil

To garnish
Cress

Method

For the Arbroath smokie
Bring the milk to a simmer in a pan and cook the Arbroath Smokie in the simmering milk for 8 minutes. Allow to cool slightly and set aside.

For the herb oil
Prepare a bowl of iced water and bring a large pan of lightly salted water to the boil. Blanch the soft herbs for 30 seconds, then lift out straight into the iced water. Leave for 5 minutes to go completely cold. Squeeze all of the excess water from the herbs and drain on a jiffy cloth. Place the drained herbs into a blender or food processor with a little of the rapeseed oil. Blend to a thick purée, then add the remaining oil. Keep blending for 5 minutes until the sides of the blender feel slightly warm. Pour the herb and oil purée through a double layer of clean muslin and allow to strain into a clean bowl; leave for 10 minutes to ensure the green oil has passed through. Place in the fridge ready for serving.

For the risotto
Heat the butter in a pan over a medium heat, add the shallot and leek, and gently sweat in the butter without colouring, then add the crushed garlic and thyme, and cook for about 10 minutes. Add the white wine and reduce until almost evaporated. Add the risotto rice followed by the stock, and occasionally stir to ensure that it does not stick or burn. Cook, stirring occasionally, for about 20 minutes until all the stock is absorbed. Slowly add the milk used to cook the smokie, one ladleful at a time, stirring constantly to allow the risotto to absorb the milk. Cook the risotto until soft. At this point, flake the cooked fish into the risotto and add the crème fraîche at the end.

For the cod
Preheat the oven to fan 180°c. Heat a non-stick sauté pan, then add a little rapeseed oil. Make sure the oil is not too hot, then add the cod loins and cook for about 3 minutes. Turn them over and place in the oven for a further 4-5 minutes until cooked. Remove from the oven and drain on a kitchen cloth.

To serve
Check the seasoning of the risotto and serve on warm plates. Place the cod loin onto the top of the risotto and garnish with the herb oil and some cress.

Rice Pudding with Drunken Raisins

This dish is dedicated to my Nana. We used to cook it together on the cold Scottish nights. My job was to stir the rice and make sure it didn't stick to the bottom of the pan, but since I joined the RN, I had to add some spirit to it – Pusser's rum.

Preparation time: 15 minutes, plus soaking | Cooking time: 25 minutes | Serves 4

Ingredients

70g raisins

Tot of Pusser's rum

1 litre organic full-fat milk

150g risotto rice

1 vanilla pod, split

25g unsalted organic butter

250ml organic single cream

35g fair-trade sugar, or to taste

Method

Soak the raisins in a tot of Pusser's rum for at least 1 hour. I prefer soaking them overnight to allow them to suck the rum in and plump up.

Add the milk, rice and split vanilla pod to the pan. Slowly bring to the boil and turn the temperature right down to cook slow, stirring in the butter to stop the rice from sticking.

Cook until the rice is soft but still has a bite; this will take about 20 minutes. When the rice becomes thick and sticky, remove from the heat.

Remove the vanilla pod from the rice and add the single cream to slacken off the mixture.

Add the sugar and return the pan to a low heat until sugar is melted; about 5 minutes. In the meantime drain the soaked raisins.

Once the sugar has melted, remove from the heat and serve. Add the raisins on top of the rice pudding and serve hot.

RECIPES
&
CHEFS
ESSENTIAL
CUISINE

Essential Cuisine

With chefs at its heart, Essential Cuisine works closely with the military, providing caterers for the Royal Navy with great-tasting, easy-to-use stocks and sauce bases, making galley life that little bit easier.

"The kitchen ethos of 'always learning' is so prevalent here, it is a pleasure to support the Navy training school, and support chefs with our products and knowledge ahead of competitions. Seeing teams constantly pushing to improve is both rewarding and humbling, knowing that our chef-to-chef advice and knowledge is respected in the industry.

We're so proud of our gluten-free stocks, jus, gravies and sauce bases. Many of our products are suitable for vegans, vegetarians and meet DOH 2017 salt guidelines. We also have a selection of ingredients that contain no declarable allergens, giving you and your brigade that added peace of mind when catering for a variety of dietary requirements.

In 2020, we were delighted to offer our best-selling foodservice products to home cooks across the nation, allowing individuals to create restaurant-quality dishes at home. These are available to purchase through a range of stockists, including Lakeland, Infusions For Chefs, Sous Chef and Henley Bridge."

The recipes here have been created by Robin Dudley, Business Development Chef, and Gary Kilminster, Business Development Manager – South West, who both have a wealth of culinary experience.

Robin started his 30-year career like most chefs, in a local restaurant aged 13. After completing a catering course at his local college in Swindon, he progressed through many restaurants throughout Wiltshire, Devon, London, Cardiff and Berkshire. Most notably, he worked on the pastry section of the world-famous Dorchester Hotel, The Greenhouse Restaurant in Mayfair, Browns 1837 under Executive Chef and mentor Andrew Turner, St David's Hotel in Cardiff, Clivedon House Hotel in Berkshire, St Michaels Manor, Queens Hotel, The Regency Hotel and The Greenway Hotel.

Gary trained at the Bournemouth & Poole College in the late 1990s and went on to acquire a wealth of experience as a chef, including positions at The De Vere Royal Bath Hotel in Bournemouth, The House of Commons in London, The De Vere Belfry in the West Midlands, Whittlebury Hall in Northampton, Suvretta House Hotel in Switzerland and as a personal chef aboard a luxury charter yacht, Masquerade of Sole in the Mediterranean. Gary has competed in over 50 competitions across the UK and abroad, winning over 35 Gold, Silver and Bronze medals and trophies.

Marinated Scallop, Fennel and Orange Salad

The main preparation for this recipe can be done in advance, either the day before or ahead of your guests arriving. This dish can be pre-plated, allowing more time for you, the host, to spend enjoying the occasion amongst friends or family.

Preparation time: 1 hour, plus marinating | Serves 4

Ingredients

For the marinated scallops
4-8 large scallops
100ml olive oil
½ star anise
1 cardamom pod
½ lime & lemon, juice and zest
¼ orange, juice and zest
¼ chilli & shallot, thinly sliced
Handful of coriander stalks
Salt and pepper

For the citrus dressing
50g sugar
50ml white wine vinegar
100ml orange juice, strained
50ml lemon juice, strained
50ml lime juice, strained

For the fennel salad
1 fennel bulb
1 orange, segmented
¼ chilli, deseeded & chopped
¼ bunch of coriander, chopped
Sea salt

For the pistachios
100g caster sugar
100g green Iranian pistachios

To garnish
Micro leaves

Method

For the marinated scallops
Clean the scallops. Warm the oil slightly and add the spices. Leave to cool. Add the oil to the rest of the ingredients, then pour over the scallops. Leave to marinate for 4-6 hours or until going slightly hard.

For the citrus dressing
Place all the dressing ingredients in a pan and cook, skimming constantly, to reduce until it has reached a coating consistency. When the dressing is clear and needs no more skimming, pour into a bottle.

For the fennel salad
Cut the fennel lengthways into 8 and slice as thinly as possible. Sprinkle with salt and leave to marinate for 2-4 hours. When soft, rinse the salt off under running water, then pat dry. Chop the orange segments up and add to the fennel. Add the chilli and coriander. Add a little of the citrus dressing. Check the seasoning, then set aside.

For the pistachios
Put the sugar in a pan and heat, without stirring, until it forms a light caramel. Pour over the pistachios and leave to cool. When hard, remove the excess sugar, then chop up to a fine crumb. Set aside.

To serve
Remove the scallops from the marinade and pat dry. Slice into 6-8. Sprinkle the pistachio crumb in a neat line. Spoon the fennel across, again in a neat line. Lay the scallop slices on the fennel. Squeeze the citrus dressing over the top and garnish with micro leaves.

Spiced Roasted Leg of Lamb

This leg of lamb is served family-style in the middle of the table with baked vegetable ratatouille, smoked garlic dauphinoise and pan jus. The dauphinoise and ratatouille can be made in advance, chilled and reheated, if you like.

Preparation time: 1 hour 15 minutes, plus marinating | Cooking time: 2 hours 20 minutes | Serves 4

Ingredients

For the lamb
55g chermoula seasoning
55g Persian seasoning
50ml rapeseed oil
1.8kg leg of lamb, boned and rolled (knuckle bone left in)

For the dauphinoise
250ml double cream & 250ml milk
3-4 smoked garlic cloves
4 sprigs of rosemary
10g butter or margarine, melted
1kg potatoes, sliced 3mm thick
Salt and white pepper

For the ratatouille
5 tbsp rapeseed oil
1 red onion, halved and sliced
3 cloves of garlic, grated
1 red & 1 yellow pepper, sliced
1 x 400g tin chopped tomatoes
1 tbsp red wine vinegar
1 tsp caster sugar
20g fresh basil & 10g oregano
1 small aubergine, sliced
1 courgette & 3 tomatoes, sliced

For the pan jus
125g Essential Cuisine Premier Veal Jus

Method

For the lamb
Mix the seasonings with the oil to form a paste. With the tip of a sharp knife make about 20 small incisions into the flesh of the lamb. Massage into the lamb, working it into the holes. Marinate for at least 4 hours in the fridge. Preheat the oven to 180°c fan. Remove the lamb from the fridge and get to room temperature. Place in a roasting tin, cover loosely with foil and roast for 2 hours, then remove the foil. Baste with the juices and return to the oven for 20 minutes for medium. Rest on a wire rack above a tray for 20–25 minutes. Wrap the lamb in the foil to keep it warm. Drain the pan of the roasting fat, retaining all the sediment.

For the dauphinoise
Preheat the oven to 140°c fan. Bring to the boil seasoned cream, milk, garlic and rosemary in a saucepan. Simmer to infuse the flavours for 5 minutes. Meanwhile, brush a serving dish with the butter and layer the potato slices, seasoning each layer. Pour the cream and milk mixture through a sieve over the potatoes, just enough to cover. Cover with foil and bake for 1-1½ hours until tender.

For the ratatouille
Preheat the oven to 140°c fan. Heat a deep sauté pan over a medium heat with oil. Add the onion and cook for 3-4 minutes until soft. Add the garlic and cook for 2-3 minutes. Add the peppers and cook for 5 minutes. Add a touch of water to prevent burning, if needed. Add the tinned tomatoes and combine well. In a separate pan, boil the vinegar and sugar until dissolved. Pour into the vegetable mix. Place a lid on the pan and turn down to low. Simmer for 10-15 minutes, or until the vegetables have softened. Season and fold in the basil and oregano. Transfer to a serving dish. Arrange the sliced aubergine, courgette and tomatoes alternately around the edges, making sure they overlap, leaving a gap in the middle. Bake for 1 hour until soft.

For the pan jus
Whisk 1l of water in a pan with the veal jus. Bring to the boil and stir for 2-3 minutes. Pour into the lamb roasting tray and deglaze. Strain into a gravy jug. Keep warm.

To serve
Serve this dish family style, placed on the table and passed around the guests.

Eton Tidy, Lemon Curd, Strawberries

This dessert is full of flavour, colour and sweetness. It acts as a great showstopper at the end of an evening of great food, wine and company with friends and family.

Preparation time: 1 hour, plus marinating | Cooking time: 4-6 hours | Serves 4

Ingredients

For the meringue
6 egg whites

300g sugar

For the marinated strawberries
200g strawberries, hulled and diced

20g sugar

4 basil leaves, chopped

For the lemon curd
2 large lemons

3 eggs

80g caster sugar

80g butter, melted

For the strawberry coulis
100g strawberries

20g sugar

For the lemon zest
50ml water

50g sugar

To garnish
400ml double cream

6 strawberries, hulled and roughly chopped

Mint leaves

Method

For the meringue
Preheat the oven to 130°c. Whisk the egg whites to soft peaks. Slowly add the sugar and keep whisking until thick. Spoon into a piping bag. Pipe the meringue into lines on a baking sheet lined with baking paper. Bake for 4-6 hours or until hard. If starting to colour, turn down the oven. When hard, remove from the oven and leave to cool. These can be stored for up to 3 days in an airtight container.

For the marinated strawberries
Mix the strawberries with the sugar and basil. Leave for 1 hour until the strawberries are soft and the sugar has dissolved. Strain, keeping the juice.

For the lemon curd
Peel the lemons and set the peel aside for later. Squeeze the lemon juice into a small pan and set aside. Whisk the eggs and the sugar in a bain marie over boiling water until thick. Heat the lemon juice and slowly add it to the egg and sugar mixture, whisking constantly. Slowly add the melted butter, whisking constantly. Leave to cool.

For the strawberry coulis
Place the berries and sugar in a bain marie over boiling water. Add the juice from the marinated strawberries and heat until the strawberries are soft. Blitz and pass through a strainer. If too thin, reduce slightly over a low heat, adding more sugar if desired. Alternatively use a thickener like Ultratex. Set aside.

For the lemon zest
Using the lemon peel saved from earlier, scrape all the white from the peel. Slice the peel as thinly as possible. Blanch for 5 seconds in boiling water, then shock in cold water. Repeat 3 times in clean water. Mix the water and sugar in a small pan and bring to the boil. Pour over the lemon zest and set aside to cool.

To serve
Whisk the double cream to soft peaks. Fold in the strained marinated strawberries and some of the curd. Crush up the meringue and fold into the cream, being careful not to over whisk. On a plate, swipe some lemon curd. Place a ring in the centre and fill with the cream mix, then carefully remove the ring. The cream should stay still. Garnish the plate with more curd, the coulis, some strawberries, lemon zest and mint.

RECIPES & CHEFS

GARY MACLEAN

Gary Maclean

Winner of MasterChef: The Professionals 2016 and Scotland's first National Chef, Gary Maclean has inspired many young people and fellow chefs in his teaching roles.

"My connection to the Royal Navy runs in the family; my grandfather signed up in the 1930s and served until 1945 so I grew up surrounded by stories about what he got up to in the war. He was also a keen photographer and we've still got an album that covers his time in the Navy, including pictures of Dunkirk. We were always really proud of him and saw him as a hero, probably reinforced by those old war movies that were always on TV when I was a kid.

It wasn't something I considered for myself, but I've always had great respect for the guys and girls who committed to protecting their country. My fascination with food started early, and like a lot of chefs I was disengaged at school but top of the class in Home Economics, encouraged by an excellent teacher to pursue cooking for a living, which I wasn't even aware you could do back then. My specialism has probably been opening high-end restaurants and I've done a lot of that, but I've also taught at the City of Glasgow College throughout my career alongside cheffing.

In 2010, going into teaching full-time was a life-changing but 100% positive move. I also proved to myself that I could achieve academically by going to university and getting my teaching qualification. The drive that made writing essays the best part of my week came from the same competitive edge I've always had, which I think is the reason behind my awards too: I always want to be the best whether it's teaching or cooking. My highlights are becoming the first Scottish National Chef in 2017 and being inducted into Scotland College's Hall of Fame for teaching. I'm also very proud of my work as a chef lecturer, and of winning MasterChef: The Professionals 2016.

I came into contact with the Navy again during a visit to the college from Rear Admiral John Clink. I suggested that we could give our students more information about careers in the Navy, because they were struggling to get young people to join as chefs. We try to open up those options to our students, because I always felt the Navy was a hidden world but one that can provide amazing futures for young people. My involvement with the Navy has actually led to my son signing up, who was destined for the RAF but after attending some events with me and meeting some important personnel, he decided it was for him. He's currently in the reserves at Glasgow, and it feels great to see a naval uniform with Maclean on again."

Potted Arbroath Smokies
with Oatcakes

This is a great but very simple dish to make and the flavour from the smokies is amazing. If you struggle getting smokies you could replace them with smoked mackerel fillets. The oatcake recipe is the one I used on the chef's table episode of MasterChef: The Professionals.

Preparation time: 30-40 minutes | Cooking time: 20-25 minutes | Serves 4

Ingredients

For the potted fish

2 Arbroath Smokies
280g cream cheese
100g crème fraîche
30g wholegrain mustard
1 banana shallot, chopped
1 bunch of chives, finely chopped
50g butter, unsalted
2 sprigs of thyme
Salt and pepper

For the oatcakes

25g plain flour
Pinch of salt
Pinch of bicarbonate of soda
110g medium oatmeal, plus extra for rolling out
25g unsalted butter
65ml boiling water

Method

For the potted fish

First, you need to prepare the fish. Start by opening the smokies up and carefully removing the back bone and the ribs. These bones should come away easily and this should separate the two fillets. Run your fingers along the flesh to feel for stray bones, removing any that you find, then peel off the skin.

Place the prepared fish into a bowl with the cream cheese, crème fraîche, mustard, shallot and chives. Add a few twists of black pepper, then mix everything together with a wooden spoon. I like a bit of texture in this so I tend not to mix it too much. Once you are happy with the texture, double check the seasoning. Once you are happy with the flavour, split the mix between your serving dishes.

Next, clarify the butter by melting it in a small saucepan and then carefully boiling until the buttermilk has evaporated and all you are left with is the oil. Allow the clarified butter to cool slightly while you pick the leaves from the thyme sprigs. Pop them into the warm butter and leave to infuse.

Make sure the surface of the potted fish is as flat as it can be, then spoon the clarified thyme butter over the top to create a thin layer, sealing the mixture in. Set in the fridge until needed.

For the oatcakes

Sift the flour, salt and bicarbonate of soda into the oatmeal. Melt the butter in the boiling water, then add the liquids to the dry ingredients. Stir until the mixture feels spongy, then turn out onto a surface scattered with oatmeal and scatter more on top.

Flatten out the dough until it's an even 0.5cm thickness all over. On MasterChef, I decided to create a hoop with the mixture at this stage. The commentator called it an oat tuile though, which is easy, whereas an oatcake hoop is very technical and difficult. You can just cut the oatcake mixture into rounds, or any way you wish, but you can try the hoop if you're feeling brave. Good luck!

Carefully transfer the oatcakes to a lined baking tray, then bake them in a preheated oven at 180°c for 15 to 20 minutes until golden. Cool on a wire rack then serve with the potted smokies.

Salmon and Quail's Egg Kedgeree

Spicy, warming and fabulous, kedgeree is always a winner. This recipe is a variant on the usual haddock, using salmon and mussels. You will need to clean and prepare the mussels, but once you have mastered this skill you might be tempted to cook mussels at home quite often!

Preparation time: 30 minutes | Cooking time: 25 minutes | Serves 4

Ingredients

300g fresh mussels
2 banana shallots, chopped
200ml white wine
50g butter
Salt and pepper, to taste
25ml vegetable oil
1 onion, sliced
1 bay leaf
1 tsp ground coriander
1 tsp ground turmeric
2 tsp curry powder
250g long grain rice
12 quail's eggs
200g hot-smoked salmon
Small bunch of flat leaf parsley, shredded
Small bunch of fresh coriander, shredded
Few sprigs of dill

Method

The first job is to clean the mussels by washing them under cold running water, using a table knife to scrape away any barnacles. You also have to remove the beards by pulling out the frilly parts that protrude from between the closed shells. If you find any mussels that are open, give them a short little tap on the side of the sink, which should encourage them to close. If they don't close, they should be thrown away as they are most likely dead.

My method for cooking mussels is to cook them very, very quickly. You'll also need a large pan with a tight-fitting lid. Place the cleaned mussels into a bowl with the chopped shallots, wine, butter, salt and pepper. Put a large pot on the heat and once hot, pour the mussel mixture in and cover with the lid. The mussels should steam in a few minutes; they are cooked once the shells are all open. Strain the mussels, but keep the cooking liquid, and pick the meat from the shells.

Heat the oil in a large pan with a tight-fitting lid and gently fry the onion for 5 minutes until softened but not coloured. Add the bay leaf and all the spices, season with salt, then continue to fry for about 3 minutes or until the mixture starts to brown and become fragrant.

Stir the rice into the spiced onions, then add 1.2 litres of water and the mussel cooking liquid. Stir and bring to the boil, then reduce to a simmer and cook with the lid on for 10 minutes.

Meanwhile, place the quail's eggs in a pan of boiling water and cook for 2.5 minutes if you would like runny egg yolks, or a little longer for hard-boiled.

Take the rice off the heat and leave to stand, still covered, for 10 to 15 minutes. The rice will be perfectly cooked if you do not lift the lid before the end of the cooking time. When it's ready, fold through the salmon, mussels and fresh herbs to make your kedgeree. Serve with the quail's eggs, peeled and quartered, on top and garnish with a few small sprigs of dill.

Coconut Panna Cotta with Pineapple Compote

Not many puddings are as refreshing or as easy as this one. The coconutty creaminess is balanced out by the tanginess of the pineapple compote, with its neat chilli kick, creating a panna cotta to die for.

Preparation time: 20 minutes | Cooking time: 10 minutes | Serves 4

Ingredients

For the panna cotta

4 x 11cm sheets of gelatine
400ml tinned coconut milk
60ml double cream
1 vanilla pod
40g caster sugar

For the pineapple compote

50g sugar
20g root ginger, finely diced
½ red chilli, finely diced
½ pineapple, finely diced or sliced

To serve

30g desiccated coconut

Method

For the panna cotta

Soak the gelatine in ice-cold water until soft, without breaking or folding the sheets. Meanwhile, put the coconut milk and cream into a pan. Split the vanilla pod lengthways, scrape out the seeds with the back of a knife, add them to the cream mixture and gently bring to the boil.

Once the mixture is boiling, take it off the heat, stir in the sugar and leave to infuse for 5 to 10 minutes. Now add the soaked gelatine, making sure you squeeze out the water first. The gelatine should be soft but intact. Let the mixture cool slightly before pouring carefully into serving moulds or small dishes, then place the panna cotta in the fridge to chill until set.

For the pineapple compote

Combine the sugar, ginger and chilli with 1 tablespoon of water in a saucepan over a medium heat and bring to the boil. When the liquid is boiling, stir in the pineapple and remove from the heat. Leave the compote to cool and chill in the fridge before use.

To serve

Toast the desiccated coconut in a hot dry pan, then let it cool and sprinkle on top of the set panna cotta with the chilled pineapple compote on the side.

RECIPES
& CHEFS

MARC
REED

Marc Reed

Royal Fleet Auxiliary Chef Marc Reed was named Royal Fleet Auxiliary Chef of the Year in 2015, an award which was presented to him by HRH Prince Edward.

"I was born in Plymouth and am still based there, with my wife Kate and our two little girls. I started cooking at the age of 16, even though I was still at school until I was 18, first in bars and cafes, followed by restaurants and hotels. I enjoyed it from such a young age, it just felt right – getting paid to do something that was enjoyable to me.

In 2010, at the age of 21, I joined the Royal Fleet Auxiliary, started my cookery course there and became class leader. From that cookery course I won Trainee Chef of the Year.

I then went to sea and started competing with the Naval Services Culinary Arts Team. In my first event I took home a bronze and a gold for my cold buffet. A career highlight in 2015 was when I was named Royal Fleet Auxiliary Chef of the Year. This was presented to me by HRH Prince Edward, which was really special. I was also recognised by the Worshipful Company of Cooks in London.

I continued with the Naval Services Culinary Arts Team and was then selected by the Combined Services Culinary Arts Team to go to the USA in 2017 and compete in Fort Lee, Virginia. I came away from there with a bronze and a silver.

I love my job. I love competing and I enjoy learning from other chefs. I would love to do some teaching in future, bring through all the young talent we've got now. Competing has changed my life, putting myself out there, fulfilling my potential, so I would love to see other people experience it. It really can be life-changing. I just didn't think I would be that good, to be honest! Being part of the Culinary Arts Team has really drawn that talent and confidence out of me.

I have always enjoyed all the different aspects of cooking; the varied nature of the job is one of my favourite things about being a chef in the Royal Fleet Auxiliary. However I am currently a baker and I do absolutely adore baking. I just love making bread, especially sourdough. It's definitely one of my favourite jobs."

Pan-seared Salmon, Beetroot, Celeriac and Horseradish

This was a dish I used for a Captain's lunch in Gdynia, Poland for the British ambassador. Having left Kiel, Germany with great-quality salmon and root vegetables, I designed this dish to showcase them.

Preparation time: 30 minutes | Cooking time: 1 hour | Serves 4

Ingredients

For the celeriac
1 whole celeriac (1-1.2kg)
300ml single cream
300ml semi-skimmed milk
Salt and pepper

For the salt-baked beetroot
100g salt & 200g plain flour
4 purple heirloom beetroots

For the candy beetroot
4 candy heirloom beetroots
50ml white wine vinegar
½ tsp black peppercorns
5g capers & 1 tsp sugar

For the horseradish butter
100g butter
Pinch of cayenne pepper
30g fresh horseradish, grated
1 lemon, juiced

For the salmon
2 tbsp cooking oil & 50g butter
4 sprigs of thyme
4 x 120-150g salmon fillets, descaled and pat-dried

For the fried leek
½ leek
Seasoned cornflour, for coating
Vegetable oil, for deep-frying

Method

For the celeriac
Preheat the oven to 180°c. Peel the celeriac and slice 5mm thick slices. Add to an ovenproof dish with the cream and milk, cover and roast for 1 hour. Purée and season.

For the salt-baked beetroot
Preheat the oven to 180°c. Make a salt dough by combining the salt, flour and a small amount of water to make a dough. Wrap the purple beetroots completely in the dough and roast for 45 minutes. Remove from the salt dough, peel and quarter.

For the candy beetroot
Peel the candy beetroot and slice into 1mm-thick slices. Cover with the white wine vinegar, peppercorns, capers, sugar and 50ml of water.

For the horseradish butter
Soften the butter and add the cayenne, horseradish and the juice of half a lemon. Reserve the remaining lemon juice for the salmon. Shape by rolling in between clingfilm to a sausage shape and chill.

For the salmon
Heat a non-stick pan, add a small amount of oil just to coat the pan, then add the thyme. Add the salmon, skin-side down, and fry for 5 minutes until almost cooked through. Turn the salmon over, add the butter and remove the pan from the heat. Baste the salmon with the butter and the salmon will finish cooking in the residual heat. Squeeze in the remaining lemon juice and season.

For the fried leek
Julienne the leek and blanch in boiling water for 10 seconds, then chill immediately in iced water. Pat dry and toss through the seasoned cornflour. Heat the vegetable oil in a pan or deep-fryer to 175°c and deep-fry the leeks for 10 seconds.

To serve
Dry the candy beetroot and portion the horseradish butter. Spoon on the celeriac purée and swoosh on the plate. Place on the salmon fillet and garnish with a quarter of salt-baked beetroot, slices of pickled candy beetroot, crispy leeks and horseradish butter.

Twice-cooked Belly Pork

Served with Savoy cabbage, pomme purée, black pudding and a cider reduction, this dish warms my heart and reminds me of my West Country roots. The crispy crackling is a winner. Start the pork the day before.

Preparation time: 1 hour, plus 1 day | Cooking time: 6 hours | Serves 4

Ingredients

For the pork
Approx. 800g belly pork
1 carrot, roughly chopped
1 onion, roughly chopped
1 fennel, roughly chopped
4 Cox's apples, roughly chopped
½ pint chicken stock
250ml cider

For the pomme purée
2 large Maris Piper or King Edward potatoes
50ml double cream
100g butter
Salt and pepper

For the cabbage
1 Savoy cabbage
50ml chicken stock
50g butter

For the black pudding
4 slices of black pudding

For the cider reduction
100ml cider
50ml double cream
50g butter

To serve
20g watercress

Method

For the pork
Preheat the oven to 140°c. Place the carrot, onion, fennel and apples in a roasting pan to act as a trivet for the belly pork. Season the pork and place it on top of the veg. Add the stock and cider, cover and roast for about 4 hours. Once the pork is cooked, reserve the cooking juices and set aside. Remove the skin, leaving as much fat on the pork as possible, and remove the bones – they should just slide out. Remove all the fat from the pork skin, sprinkle the skin with a little salt and leave to dry out for 12 hours whilst the pork belly cools in the fridge.

For the pomme purée
Preheat the oven to 180°c. Roast the potatoes for 1 hour. When the potatoes are cooked, peel them and place the crispy skins into the cream to infuse for 10 minutes. Remove the skins and add the flesh of the potatoes, putting them through a ricer. Mix and season, then finish with butter and a little milk if needed.

For the pork
Preheat the oven to 180°c. Portion the belly pork and place in an ovenproof dish with the reserved cooking liquor (removing the fat) and cook for 1 hour. Heat a deep-fryer to 175°c and cook the pork belly skin until crispy. Season with salt and crack into pieces.

For the cabbage
Chiffonade the Savoy cabbage and braise in the chicken stock and butter.

For the black pudding
Warm the black pudding through in an oven.

For the cider reduction
Remove the juices from the pork, add the cider and reduce, then add the double cream. Cool slightly and add the butter to finish the sauce.

To serve
Spoon on the creamy mash potato and drag with your spoon, then add your pork belly to the plate. Add the braised cabbage and black pudding, pour on the sauce and top with some fresh peppery watercress and the crispy crackling.

Raspberry, Pistachio and Baked White Chocolate Layered Parfait

A childhood classic I adapted and developed to be able to make on board a ship for large numbers. This no-churn recipe is still a challenge, but it is worth the effort. Make this dessert the day before.

Preparation time: 1 hour, plus overnight cooling | Cooking time: 20 minutes | Serves 4-6

Ingredients

200g white chocolate
100g caster sugar
3 egg yolks
150g raspberries
20ml glucose syrup
75g pistachios
1 vanilla pod
300g double cream
100ml condensed milk

Method

Preheat the oven to 170°c. Bake the white chocolate on a non-stick tray, stirring regularly to ensure it doesn't burn – you're looking for a caramel or sand colour. It will look grainy but don't worry. Smooth the white chocolate out on silicone paper to make thin sheets of chocolate for layering.

Put the sugar in a pan and bring it to 121°c. As it is heating, whip the egg yolks. Once the sugar has reached the temperature, add it slowly onto the whipped egg yolks, whisking to make a sabayon. It should be pale white in colour.

Add half of the raspberries to the glucose syrup in a pan, and boil to make a coulis. Strain and set aside.

Toast the pistachios and crush half of them. Set aside.

Scrape the seeds from the vanilla pod into the cream and whip to soft peaks. Fold the condensed milk and sabayon into the cream. Divide the mixture between two bowls. Add the coulis to one. Add the crushed pistachios to the other.

Assemble the parfait in a lined 450g/1lb loaf tin, layering each flavour cream and the shards of white chocolate. Once the tin is full, wrap in cling film and freeze overnight.

To serve

Remove the parfait from the tin and cut into slices. Serve with the rest of the fresh raspberries and the whole toasted pistachios.

RECIPES
&
CHEFS
MARK
PENLINGTON

Mark Penlington

After a short but illustrious naval career, Mark Penlington achieved his goal of working in a fine dining restaurant kitchen at the now-Michelin-starred Alchemilla.

"My interest in food started early - mostly in the form of experimenting with microwaved scrambled eggs as a kid, which I'm sure were absolutely disgusting! - but it was going to work in a local pub that really ignited my passion for cooking. I hated school because I loved being hands-on and the learning style just didn't allow for that, so taking a work-based NVQ allowed me to see that I could go on to better things. After that first qualification, I went into rosette-level dining but was keen to explore different cultures and cuisines. I figured working in the Royal Navy would be a brilliant way to see the world while being paid to work, as well as learning so much more about food.

I joined up in 2011 and experienced so many career highlights over the following years. I loved cooking on board ships when the captains were hosting dinners for important guests, and also had the opportunity to cook for dinner parties on the HMS Victory, Nelson's flagship. Representing the Navy in competitions was always exciting too; I was part of the team who achieved the highest ever score at a culinary competition for the armed forces. I was also picked to be part of another team who cooked within the Royal Household for a short time, helping to cater for events at Buckingham Palace.

After leaving the Royal Navy, I went straight into working at Alchemilla with Alex Bond. They created a position for me once I'd completed a stage (an internship in another chef's kitchen) to get back into civilian cooking and I worked there for a year. I love fine dining and had always wanted to work in that environment, so that felt like a huge achievement for me, especially because the restaurant has since been awarded a Michelin star. My biggest passion is probably simple food done really well though; after Alchemilla I was very keen to open my own place and go for a star by cooking highly elevated pub-style food. However, I had to weigh up the work-life balance, having already spent a lot of time away from home during my naval career.

I now deliver training and apprenticeships for a company called HIT Training who work with young people wanting to become chefs. I've come full circle in that sense, because my own apprenticeship had a profound effect on me and altered the whole direction of my future. At the moment I'm really enjoying working with the trainees, being right at the forefront and still getting to cook, as well as having weekends off which still feels like a novelty!"

Cured Sea Trout with Buttermilk Sauce

I have chosen to showcase sea trout in this dish, as it's something that often gets overlooked or replaced by salmon, both in restaurants and at home. This recipe is a great example of a really tasty alternative.

Preparation time: 12 hours | Cooking time: 10 minutes | Serves 4

Ingredients

250g coarse sea salt

250g sugar

2 lemons, zested

1 lime, zested

1 x 500-600g sea trout, skinned and pin-boned

50g pumpkin seeds

20g black sesame seeds

For the buttermilk sauce

700g buttermilk

250g butter

150g milk

2 lemons, juiced

2g xanthan gum

For the chive oil

200g chives

500ml vegetable oil

Method

Combine the salt, sugar and citrus zest then spread half the mixture onto a large tray. Place the trout on top and cover with the remaining cure. Cover with cling film and refrigerate for 12 hours. The fish should feel firm to the touch, so if it is still soft after 12 hours return it to the fridge for another few hours. When it's ready, brush off the cure and wash the fish in cold water.

Place the pumpkin and black sesame seeds on a baking tray and bake in the oven (fan off) at 160°c for 5 to 8 minutes, until popping and golden, then crush them lightly with a pestle and mortar. Serve them scattered over the cured fish with the sauce and oil below.

For the buttermilk sauce

Warm the buttermilk and butter in a pan, but do not let the mixture boil. Transfer to a blender and add the milk, lemon juice and xanthan gum. Blend for 2 minutes.

For the chive oil

Blend the chives and oil together in a blender for around 5 minutes, then leave the mixture to strain through muslin cloth into a bowl overnight in the fridge.

Beef & Onion

This dish features braised ox cheeks, onions three ways - roasted whole, caramelised onion purée and crispy shallots - smoked potato and a bone marrow sauce.

Preparation time: 2 hours | Cooking time: 4-5 hours | Serves 4

Ingredients

4 ox cheeks
1 large onion
2 carrots
1 stick of celery
Vegetable oil
250ml white wine
2 litres beef stock
1 bunch of thyme

For the onions

7 large white onions
100ml double cream
3 shallots

For the smoked potato

4 handfuls of fresh hay
150ml double cream
400g ratte potatoes
100g butter

For the sauce

20g pickled parsley stalks
1 bunch of chives
1 shallot
100g bone marrow
300g demi-glace
Dash of sherry vinegar

Method

Trim the fat from the ox cheeks. Peel and chop the vegetables. Heat a pan, add 3 tbsp of vegetable oil and caramelise the cheeks all over, seasoning with salt. Remove from the pan, add the vegetables, reduce the heat and sweat for 5 minutes. Remove the vegetables, deglaze the pan with the white wine then pour into a deep dish. Place the ox cheeks and vegetables into the dish with the beef stock and thyme. Cover with foil and braise at 160°c for 4 hours, turning halfway through. Once tender, leave to cool. Strain the liquid from the pan and save for the sauce, discarding the vegetables.

For the onions

Peel 4 onions, leaving the root on to maintain shape. Heat a pan and add 2 tbsp of vegetable oil. Season with salt and place into the pan root side up. Once caramelised, place the onions onto a tray and roast at 180°c for 20 minutes, or until soft. Peel and chop 3 more onions and heat a heavy-based pan. Add the chopped onions and stir every 5 minutes or so, scraping the bottom of the pan with a spatula. Cook over a medium heat until dark golden brown; this will take up to an hour. If the pan starts to catch, reduce the heat and add a splash of water, cleaning the bottom. Once caramelised, add the double cream and blend to a purée. Pass this through a sieve for a smooth consistency and season with salt. Heat 500ml of vegetable oil in a deep frying pan. Julienne the shallots, then fry them in the hot oil until crispy. Drain on paper towels and season. Store in an airtight jar until ready to serve.

For the smoked potato

Place the hay into a lidded fireproof pot. Pour the cream into a metal bowl and place on top of the hay. Set fire to the hay and place the lid on the pot. The flames will be extinguished, creating smoke. Leave for 10 minutes, then stir the cream and repeat this process until it has taken on a smoky flavour. Peel the potatoes and boil them in salted water until soft, then press through a ricer. Heat the smoked cream and butter together. Slowly incorporate this mixture into the mashed potato until smooth. Season.

For the sauce

Chop the pickled parsley stalks and chives (keeping them separate). Brunoise your shallot. Dice the cold bone marrow into 1cm chunks. Add the ox cheek cooking liquid to the demi-glace in a pan and simmer. Add the parsley stalks and sherry vinegar, then the shallot and salt to taste. Finish with the bone marrow and chives, then serve the sauce immediately with your dish.

Nuts About Chocolate

Chocolate fondant became one of my favourite desserts when I first got the opportunity to work with fresh food on the dessert section of Lambs at the Market in Mansfield. I fell in love with cooking the moment I tasted this. My motivation to progress as a chef started here.

Preparation time: 1 hour 30 minutes | Cooking time: 30 minutes | Serves 6

Ingredients

For the hazelnut ice cream
180g hazelnuts
260g milk
130g double cream
65g brown sugar
½ tsp salt
2 tbsp hazelnut liqueur

For the hazelnut tuile
20g blanched almonds
20g blanched hazelnuts
50g sugar
15g butter, softened
15g 00 flour
1 egg white
1 drop of vanilla extract

For the chocolate fondant
125g unsalted butter
125g dark chocolate (70% cocoa solids)
125g caster sugar
4 whole eggs
4 egg yolks
75g plain flour
Cocoa powder, for dusting

Method

For the hazelnut ice cream

Preheat the oven to 150°c. Tip the hazelnuts onto a lined baking sheet and roast for 10 to 12 minutes until golden brown. Meanwhile, pour the milk, cream, half of the sugar and the salt into a heavy-based saucepan. Bring to a simmer and heat gently for 6 minutes, then set aside.

While they are still warm, rub the roasted hazelnuts in a clean tea towel to remove the skins. Tip 130g of the skinned hazelnuts into a food processor with the remaining brown sugar and liqueur, then blend for about 4 minutes until you have a smooth paste. Add the hazelnut paste to the cream mixture and place the pan over a low heat, then simmer for 5 minutes until the paste has dissolved.

Pour the hazelnut cream into a bowl or jug and allow to cool, then transfer to an ice cream machine and churn until smooth. Serve immediately as soft scoop ice cream, or freeze until needed and remove 5 minutes before serving. Blend the remaining 50g of hazelnuts into a crumb for serving.

For the hazelnut tuile

Preheat the oven to 180°c while you blitz the nuts in a food processor. Add the sugar, butter and flour and blitz again until fully incorporated. Add the egg white and vanilla, then blend until the mixture is loose and spreadable. Place teaspoons of the mixture onto a large baking sheet lined with greaseproof paper. Use the back of the spoon to spread them out into a very thin, neat circles, leaving space between each one. Bake the tuiles in the preheated oven for 7 to 10 minutes until golden around the edges. Shape while warm and then leave to cool.

For the chocolate fondant

Melt the butter and chocolate together in a metal bowl over a saucepan of boiling water, not letting the water touch the bottom of the bowl. Whisk the sugar, eggs and yolks together until light, fluffy and pale in colour. Gently fold in the melted butter and chocolate, then the flour. Place the mixture into ramekins or pots dusted with cocoa powder and refrigerate for 4 hours until set. Preheat the oven to 200°c and bake the fondants for 11 minutes. Remove from the oven and turn them out of the ramekins if you like, but be careful not to break the fondant. Serve immediately with your hazelnut ice cream, tuile and crumb on the side.

RECIPES
& CHEFS
MATTIE TEW

Mattie Tew

Mattie Tew was responsible for bringing all the contributing chefs together for this book, in order to share their stories and recipes from their careers in the Royal Navy and beyond.

"I was never really well-behaved or academic at school; I had no clear direction and a lot of negativity from my teachers. I joined the Royal Navy in September 1999 at the age of 16 from my home in Warwickshire and quickly established my passion for cooking by competing at the Joint Services Salon Culinaire while in training, and achieving outstanding results as a young chef.

During my service, I have been lucky enough to have served in Aircraft Carriers, Type 42 and 45 Destroyers, Type 23 Frigates and Minesweepers. I've also travelled the globe, visiting over 60 countries and achieving over 3,500 sea days in the process... and I'm not done yet! I have contributed to shore establishments around the UK, including Commander in Chief Fleet, London, The Old Naval Academy and the Second Sea Lords residence, Portsmouth.

I've completed operational tours of Iraq and Afghanistan, and was also part of the decompression team in Cyprus for 3 Commando Brigade returning from OP Herrick. One particular highlight of my career was working for my beloved Harlequins Rugby Team, where I helped write and execute menus with diet and nutritional needs for international players.

In 2015 I was awarded the Apprenticeships Champion award for contribution to apprenticeships within the Royal Navy. As a very keen competition chef, I competed for the Royal Navy at the Inter-services Exercise Joint Caterer, Salon Culinaire at Hotelympia (HRC) and ScotHot. I am a member of the Combined Services Culinary Arts Team and have represented the UK and the British Military at the World Culinary Olympics in Stuttgart, Germany.

As part of my last job with the Royal Navy Presentation Team, I was lucky enough to visit schools, colleges and international food shows up and down the British Isles, to talk about and to demonstrate my role as a chef within the Royal Navy. I found this to be not only interesting, but, more importantly, very worthwhile. These students could be our future.

I feel that I've achieved so much during my time, but I'd replace all my achievements to simply watch the people I've helped along the way succeed for themselves.

I am now an advanced craft instructor at the Defence College of Logistics and Policing, Worthy Down, training potential leaders of the future Royal Navy. I live in Winchester with my wife Lauran and our five children Kyle, Isobella, Harry, Isla and Harper, without whom I wouldn't have been able to achieve any of my goals and dreams. In my spare time (not that I get much as a chef) I am a passionate rugby player, coach and fan."

Haly and Butte

Inspired by Escoffier and his genius cooking style of basic but classic dishes, I have taken soft poached halibut with a mustard beurre blanc using chicken stock, which is very fashionable at the moment, and then simply served this with baby leeks and white shimeji mushrooms, garnishing with sea fennel.

Preparation time: 30 minutes | Cooking time: 30-45 minutes | Serves 4

For the poached halibut
200g sea salt
200g sugar
4 x 140g halibut fillets
100ml Champagne

For the beurre blanc
100g shallots, finely chopped
A little salted butter, for cooking
240ml dry white wine
80ml chicken stock
160ml double cream
200g unsalted butter
2 tsp wholegrain mustard
Salt and pepper

For the leeks
A little salted butter, for cooking
4 baby leeks, finely chopped

For the mushrooms
A little salted butter, for cooking
100g white shimeji mushrooms, cleaned

To serve
Sea fennel

For the poached halibut

Preheat the water bath to a temperature of 42°c. Combine the salt and sugar in a bowl. Using a sharp knife, cut the halibut fillets into neat squares. Lightly coat the fillets with the salt and sugar mixture and leave for 10 minutes to cure.

Using a vacpac, seal the cured halibut fillets inside individual vacuum bags (1 fillet per bag), adding one-quarter of the Champagne to each bag before sealing. Place the bags in the water bath and leave to cook sous vide for 10 minutes. Once cooked, remove the fillets from the bags and reserve the poaching liquid.

For the beurre blanc

Sweat off the shallots with some salted butter. Add the white wine and reduce by half. Add the stock and halibut poaching liquor and again reduce by half. Add the cream and cook to get the required consistency. Remove from the heat and beat in the unsalted butter, mustard and seasoning. Keep warm but do not boil.

For the leeks

Using a medium frying pan, melt the butter quickly and fry the leeks until soft.

For the mushrooms

At the same time in a different pan, melt the butter quickly and sauté the shimeji mushrooms over a medium heat. When they become tender, add them into the beurre blanc.

To serve

Coat the bottom of the dish with a thin layer of the beurre blanc, pile the leeks in the centre, then add some of the white shimeji mushrooms and more sauce. Finish with the poached halibut and a garnish of sea fennel.

It's All About The Lamb

For my lamb dish, I wanted to make it exactly what it says on the tin... LAMB. Not to be bogged down with purées, gels and torched bits 'n' bobs, but simply, lamb. I chose this dish to marry unique flavours that are not always associated with red meat.

I live in Hampshire, so I got in touch with a local breeder and farmer near Ripley in Hampshire. Following an interesting discussion, I discovered that their New Zealand Romney lambs give a taste like no other. Having taken ownership of a whole lamb, I experimented with the whole carcass, using the cheaper (rarely used) cuts, rather than the more mainstream cuts you see in restaurants.

So... I used the loin from the saddle, and a sticky glaze of Dijon mustard and Hampshire honey. I kept the freshness with some herbs to bring that lamb back to the pasture.

The lamb's sweetbreads were brined in ewe's milk, again with fresh herbs, before they go into a hot pan and are basted in that lovely foaming butter, plenty of seasoning and a drizzle of jus.

To make the faggot, I used the belly with some of the fat and some of the lamb's liver, kidney and neck, with the addition of a brunoise of vegetables, anchovy and wild garlic, which I foraged from a field in Knowle near Fareham. The anchovy brings an umami flavour to marry it all together. The faggots are wrapped in the lamb's caul, and basted during the cooking process with stock.

I handpicked the asparagus (with a little help from my children) from a farm in Petersfield, Hampshire. It is blanched in juiced asparagus and plunged into iced water for service. It's finished in a pan with asparagus butter and seasoned with asparagus salt. It may be just a piece of asparagus, but I wanted to intensify the flavour, as every element on the plate is as important as the main piece.

What better to go with lamb and asparagus than some hand-picked morels from the South Downs national park, lightly sautéed in butter and seasoned with cep salt.

I love making a good clean sauce, and this dish is no different. I add some balsamic vinegar to the stock to create a piquant taste to cut through the fatty lamb. Lamb wouldn't be complete without mint, so I also added just enough mint for the flavour come through.

The pickled sweet shallot petals bring an extra kick on the taste buds; their piquant flavour will cut through some of the richness of this dish.

Plating is important. Get the lamb on the plate... That is what it's all about! I garnished it with wilted wild garlic, wild garlic flowers and garlic chives. Plate however you want to, everyone has different styles – let the food do the talking. I hope you have enjoyed reading about my dish as much as I enjoyed creating and eating it.

It's All About The Lamb

Herb-rolled Hampshire-bred lamb loin, lamb sweetbreads, anchovy and wild garlic lamb faggot, asparagus, morels, wilted wild garlic, pickled sweet shallot pearls served with a balsamic and mint jus, and garnished with wild garlic flowers and garlic chives.

Preparation time: 24 hours | Cooking time: 45 minutes | Serves 4

For the lamb loin
4 lamb loins
25g unsalted butter
1 tsp Dijon mustard
1 tsp honey
1 tsp Essential Cuisine lamb glace
2 sprigs of mint, finely chopped
1 bunch of parsley, chopped
3 wild garlic leaves, finely chopped

For the sweetbreads
20g lamb's sweetbreads
1 pint ewe's milk
3 sprigs of rosemary
3 sprigs of thyme
Smoked garlic salt
25g unsalted butter
1 tbsp jus

For the jus
Essential Cuisine lamb stock
100ml white balsamic vinegar
4 sprigs of mint

For the faggots
5g each lamb kidney, liver, belly and neck
200ml ewe's milk
3 anchovy fillets
3g each carrot, celery and

For the lamb loin
Trim off the excess fat and sinew, wrap tightly in cling film and leave to hang in the fridge overnight.

For the sweetbreads
Portion the sweetbreads into the required size. Soak in the ewe's milk and herbs in the refrigerator overnight.

For the jus
Mix and wet down the Essential Cuisine lamb stock and begin to reduce.

For the faggots
Skin the kidney and liver, then soak for a couple of hours in the ewe's milk. Discard the soaking liquid, wash in fresh water and dry. Use a mincer to combine the neck, belly, liver, kidney and anchovies. Brunoise the vegetables and lightly sauté until translucent. Once cooled, add the vegetables to the minced lamb mixture. Incorporate the lamb glace and the wild garlic. Weigh into 8g balls and cover in the caul. Place onto a lined tray and refrigerate.

For the asparagus
Trim and peel 3 sticks of asparagus, 5cm long, per plate. Blanch in boiling salted water and then refresh in iced water. Cut the remaining asparagus into pieces and feed through a juicer; retain in the fridge. Combine the asparagus juice with the unsalted butter and refrigerate.

For the pickled sweet shallot petals
Peel and halve the shallots, then trim so that you have petals. Combine the pickling ingredients together and bring to the boil. Remove from the heat and allow to cool. Scorch the pearls on a flame to give a charred appearance to the inner. Add the shallot petals to the cooled pickle and set aside in the fridge for 15 minutes. Take them out of the pickling liquor and set aside ready for service.

For the jus
Add the balsamic vinegar and mint, and warm the sauce. Keep stirring and tasting until it takes on just enough minty-ness then remove the leaves. Keep warm.

It's All About The Lamb contd...

shallot

1 tsp Essential Cuisine lamb glace

3 wild garlic leaves, finely chopped

Lamb's caul

50g unsalted butter

1 tbsp jus

For the asparagus

1 bunch of asparagus, trimmed

50g unsalted butter

For the pickled sweet shallot petals

1-2 shallots

200ml sherry vinegar

10g kosher salt

10g caster sugar

10 white peppercorns

2 star anise

5 juniper berries

For the morels

25g unsalted butter

4-5 morels, brushed clean

Cep salt

To garnish

Wild garlic leaves, garlic flowers and garlic chives

For the faggots

Preheat the oven to 170°c. Place the faggots on a lined baking tray and cook in the oven for 4-5 minutes. Heat a mini frying pan, add the butter, then add the faggots and jus, and baste in the jus and foaming butter.

For the sweetbreads

In another small pan, heat a little oil. Add the sweetbread and season with the smoked garlic salt. Add the butter and jus, basting as you go.

For the lamb loin

Add a little oil to a hot pan, then add the loin and season with salt. Add the butter and baste when foaming. When you have dark colouring on the lamb, remove from the pan. Combine the Dijon, honey and lamb glace, and use to paint the top of the lamb. Trim the ends and roll the top in the finely chopped herbs before allowing to rest.

For the asparagus

Bring 1 pint of salted water to the boil and add the asparagus butter. Plunge the asparagus in for roughly 1 minute.

For the morels

Heat the butter until foaming, and toss in the morels. Remove and season with the cep salt. In the same pan as the morels, flash the wild garlic leaves for the garnish for 3-4 seconds.

To serve

Plate up the loin, sweetbreads, faggots, asparagus, morels, wild garlic leaves and pickled shallot petals. Garnish with wild garlic flowers and garlic chives. Spoon the jus over the faggot.

Salted Caramel Tart and Gingerbread Ice Cream

I have finished this dessert with a honeycomb macaron, the recipe for which you will find on the next page.

Preparation time: 60 minutes | Cooking time: 60 minutes | Serves 6

For the pastry case
190g plain flour
40g icing sugar
2 tsp kosher salt
120g unsalted butter, cold
1 large egg yolk
2 tsp double cream
½ tsp vanilla extract

For the salted caramel filling
240g double cream
5 tbsp unsalted butter
1 tsp kosher salt to taste
2 tsp vanilla extract
300g granulated sugar
85g light syrup
63g water

For the gingerbread ice cream
450ml milk
300ml double cream
1 vanilla pod, with seeds scraped
500ml sugar syrup
9 egg yolks
4g ice cream stabiliser
200g gingerbread, stale

For the caramel shard
Werther's Originals

To serve
Honeycomb macaron (see next page)

For the pastry case
Place the flour, sugar and salt in the bowl of a food processor. Pulse in the butter until the mixture resembles breadcrumbs. Add the egg yolk, cream and vanilla, and process until the dough gathers into a ball and pulls away from the sides. Wrap in cling film, and chill for 1 hour. Preheat the oven to 190°c. On a floured surface, roll out the dough to 3mm, and press into a 23cm tart pan, trimming any excess. Prick the pastry and bake in the oven for 18-22 minutes, or until set and turning golden at the edge.

For the salted caramel filling
Gently heat the cream, butter and salt until the butter has melted and the salt has dissolved. Remove from heat and add the vanilla. In a larger pan, combine the sugar, syrup and water over a medium-high heat, swirling the pan occasionally. Continue to boil the sugar mixture until the bubbles get smaller and it becomes amber-coloured. Reduce the heat to low, and pour in the cream mixture, whisking constantly. Simmer until it reaches 118°c on a sugar thermometer. Pour the caramel into the pastry case.

For the gingerbread ice cream
Combine the milk, cream and vanilla pod in a pan and bring to the boil. Remove from the heat and leave to infuse for 30 minutes. Bring the sugar syrup to the boil, then reduce the heat and simmer for 10 minutes. Add the egg yolks to a food processor and add the syrup gradually, followed by the infused milk and cream mixture. Once combined, add the stabiliser. Set the Thermomix to 80°c, add the mixture and process for 8 minutes at speed 4. Alternatively, bring to 80°c in a pan, stirring continuously while taking care not to scramble the mix. Transfer to a bowl set over iced water and keep stirring until cool. Transfer to an ice cream maker and, while the blade is moving, crumble in the gingerbread, reserving some to serve. Remove from the churner once ready and place into a sealable container. Freeze until required.

For the caramel shard
Preheat the oven to 180°c. Place the sweets on a silpat mat and onto a tray. Bake for 8 minutes, or until they melt and form air bubbles. Cool, then put in an airtight container.

To serve
Use some of the reserved gingerbread as a carrier for the ice cream to stop it moving on the plate. Stand the macaron upright. Place a slice of the tart off centre. Place the ice cream on the crumb and use the caramel shard to give the plate some height.

Honeycomb Macaron

These delicate macarons are used to finish off the dessert on the previous page, but are also wonderful served on their own.

Preparation time: 50 minutes | Cooking time: 20 minutes | Serves 20

For the almond base
300g ground almonds
300g icing sugar
110g egg white

For the Italian meringue
110g egg white
55g water
300g caster sugar
1g yellow food gel
1g brown food gel

For the caramel filling
175g butter
175g caster sugar
120g golden syrup
397g condensed milk (1 tin)

For the honeycomb
200g caster sugar
70g glucose
45g honey
25g water
10g bicarbonate of soda

For the almond base
Add the ground almonds, icing sugar and egg white to the bowl of a food mixer and whisk to combine. Set aside until required.

For the Italian meringue
Whisk the egg white on a low speed. Add the water and 280g of the caster sugar to a pan and place over a medium-high heat. When the sugar mixture reaches 105°c on a sugar thermometer, add the remaining 20g of caster sugar to the egg whites to stabilise the meringue. Increase the speed. When the sugar has reached 118°c (or 'soft ball' stage), remove the pan from the heat, reduce the speed of the food mixer and drizzle the sugar down the side of the bowl into the egg white. Increase the speed, whisk for 1 minute, then stop. Add the food colourings and whisk on medium until the meringue has cooled to body temperature and is glossy and smooth.

For the macaron shells
Mix one-third of the Italian meringue into the ground almond base until smooth and incorporated. Repeat this twice more until the two mixtures are combined and you have a smooth, shiny meringue. Transfer the meringue to a piping bag with a 1cm nozzle, then pipe 4.5cm circles onto a baking tray lined with silicone paper, or directly onto a silicone baking mat. Set aside to allow a skin to form; about 30 minutes. Preheat the oven to 130°c. Cook the macarons for 17-18 minutes, until just peeling away from the baking mat. Cool before pairing the halves according to size.

For the caramel filling
Place the ingredients for the filling into a pan and place over a low heat. Stir constantly for around 10 minutes or until the caramel has turned a nice dark golden colour and started to thicken. Place the caramel in the fridge to cool. Once it is nearly set, transfer to a piping bag ready to fill the macarons.

For the honeycomb
Heat the caster sugar, glucose, honey and water in a pan until it reaches 150°c on a sugar thermometer. Remove from the heat and quickly whisk in the bicarbonate of soda. Allow it to cook and rise for 1 minute, then pour out onto a lined tray. Cool completely. Break the honeycomb into small pieces, saving a few for decoration.

To serve
Pipe a blob of the caramel onto the flat side of one macaron shell, press a piece of the honeycomb into the centre and then press the paired shell onto the top.

RECIPES & CHEFS

NICK VADIS

Nick Vadis

Chef instructor Nick Vadis is passionate about giving young people the best opportunities to thrive in catering careers and has been involved in numerous culinary competitions as a participant, mentor and coach.

"I joined the Royal Navy in 1974 as a helicopter mechanic because somebody in a careers office thought I had the qualifications to be 'so much more' than a chef. I was almost coerced into the role, but it wasn't what I really wanted, so after basic training I requested to recategorise and become a chef like my father had been. I managed to go to HMS Pembroke and complete my training at the cookery school. From then, I never really looked back. In the mid-70s joining the Navy was a very attractive prospect, partly because the opportunities to travel were much greater in those days, as we had a bigger Navy then and ships went all round the world.

I advanced quickly and was always keen to get on; I was promoted to Leading Hand at 21. It was during my advanced chef's course that I was asked whether I'd ever contemplated being a cookery instructor. It had never crossed my mind before, even though my mother was a teacher, and in fact I laughed at them for asking then forgot about it during the following seven month deployment to America. On returning, I was drafted back to a shore establishment and it was there the offer started to resonate with me. I started to think that maybe I could do something different within the Navy and teaching was becoming an interest of mine.

Fast-forward 16 years, and I found myself as the

Warrant Officer with a degree in teaching running the Royal Naval Cookery School, whereby I'd now combined both my parents' jobs in mine. During that time, my interest in competing was piqued by a certain display cabinet full of gold medals at the cookery school. Ever since a conversation about it with the then-Warrant Officer, Ken Fraser, who incidentally had competed in the England National Team many years before, I've been involved in competitions as competitor, coach or mentor for numerous culinary teams from the Combined Service to the Craft Guild of Chefs, and finally as a competitor and coach to the England National Team.

I decided to leave the services after what I can only describe as 25 brilliant years, and step into civvy street. What I've taken with me are many career highlights, from international awards to honorary professorship, as well as my true passion for engaging with the next generation. We can take a lot out of this industry, but unless we give back the future doesn't look too great, so for me it's all about mentoring the next generation of chefs and giving them some of the opportunities that I had."

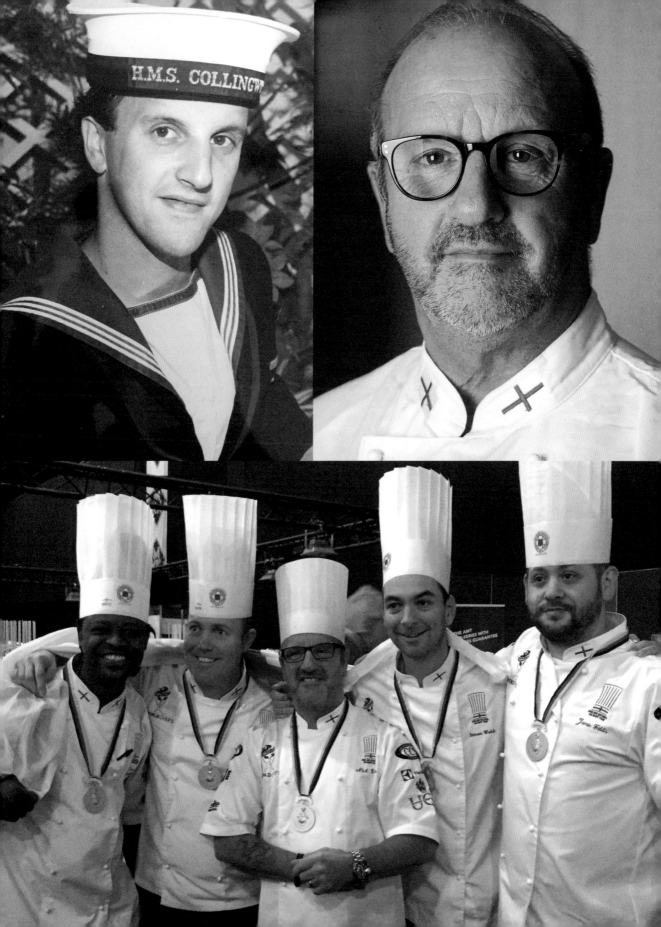

Baked Sea Bream with
Herb Crumb

Served with braised fennel, tomatoes and a warm caper dressing, this dish is light but full of flavour.

Preparation time: 20 minutes | Cooking time: 40 minutes | Serves 4

Ingredients

1kg fennel bulb

20g capers

30g shallots, finely diced

70ml white wine vinegar

50ml olive oil

1 lemon, zested and juiced

Salt and pepper

4 ripe vine tomatoes

4 fillets of sea bream

20g flat leaf parsley

80g panko breadcrumbs

Method

Preheat the oven to 180°c. Cut the fennel lengthways through the root, then trim out the tough core. Place the fennel into a small ovenproof dish with the capers, shallots, white wine vinegar, olive oil, lemon juice, salt and pepper.

Place the dish into the preheated oven and cook the fennel for about 30 minutes, checking after 20 to see whether it is softening. Once cooked, keep warm to one side. Leave the oven on.

Quarter and deseed the tomatoes, chop the parsley and remove the skin from the sea bream fillets if this hasn't been done already. Add half the parsley to the braised fennel.

To make the herb crumb, simply mix the remaining parsley with the lemon zest and breadcrumbs. Season with salt and pepper to taste, then coat the fish fillets in the crumb and drizzle with a little olive oil. Lay them carefully on a baking tray, then bake in the oven for about 10 minutes until they are just cooked through.

To serve

Spoon some of the braised fennel and caper mixture into a dish or bowl, add the tomatoes, place the crumbed sea bream on top, then drizzle some of the fennel cooking liquor over and around the dish.

Roasted Wood Pigeon

This rich and hearty main course is served with date purée, cauliflower and macadamia cream, potatoes cooked with confit leg meat, Savoy cabbage and butter beans.

Preparation time: 1 hour | Cooking time: 2 hours | Serves 4

Ingredients

200g dried dates
100ml Port
250g cauliflower
200g macadamia nuts
150ml milk
50g butter
4 pigeons
200ml duck fat
12 cloves of garlic
Small sprig of thyme
200g potatoes
50ml double cream
1 Savoy cabbage
60g cooked butter beans
Salt and pepper

Method

First, make the date purée by simmering the dates in the Port until softened. Transfer to a food processor and blend until smooth. Adjust the consistency by adding water if needed.

Cut the cauliflower into small pieces and place in a pan with 150g of the macadamia nuts, the milk and a little salt. Boil until the cauliflower is cooked, then transfer the solids to a food processor, reserving the milk. Blend until smooth, adding 30g of the butter and enough of the reserved milk to get a creamy consistency. It should be soft, light and just hold up on the plate.

Remove the legs from the pigeons and melt the duck fat in a pan over a low to medium heat. Place the pigeon legs, remaining macadamias, garlic cloves and thyme into the fat and cook gently for 20 minutes to confit. Leave to cool slightly and preheat the oven to 180°c.

Thinly slice the potatoes using a mandoline and layer them in an ovenproof dish, seasoning and brushing with a little of the duck fat as you go. About halfway through, flake the confit leg meat over the potatoes, pour in half of the cream until it finds its own level, then finish layering the potatoes. Add more cream as required to just below the surface of the potatoes.

Cover the dish with foil and bake in the preheated oven for 45 minutes. Remove the foil for the last 15 minutes and test with a skewer to see if the potatoes are soft all the way through. Place something heavy on top of the dish to press them and leave in the fridge. Turn the oven temperature up to 220°c.

Heat a little oil in a roasting tin, add the remaining butter, then sear the pigeons carefully on all sides just until coloured. Roast in the hot oven for about 7 to 10 minutes, then rest for 10 minutes. Meanwhile, cut the potato bake into slices and pan fry them in a little butter to reheat. Sauté the confit garlic and macadamia nuts in the same pan. Shred and cook the cabbage briefly in boiling water, then drain well. Pour the pigeon pan juices into a small saucepan and simmer until reduced to a sauce consistency. Add the butter beans to heat through.

To serve

Place all the accompaniments on the plate, carve the pigeon breasts and place on top of the potato slice, then drizzle everything with the reduced pigeon jus.

White Chocolate Panna Cotta
with Florentines

This delicate dessert looks impressive but is surprisingly straightforward to make. If you don't have a silicone baking mat for the florentines, a baking tray lined with good quality greaseproof paper will work just as well.

Preparation time: 30 minutes, plus 2 hours chilling | Cooking time: 20 minutes | Serves 4

Ingredients

For the panna cotta
1 vanilla pod
2½ leaves of gelatine
500ml double cream
100g caster sugar
50g white chocolate

For the florentines
100g butter
400g sugar
10g flour
100g mixed nuts (walnuts, nibbed almonds, macadamias and pecans all work well)
Splash of lemon juice

Method

For the panna cotta
Split the vanilla pod in half lengthways and soak the gelatine in cold water until softened. Heat the cream and vanilla in a pan, then add the sugar and stir gently until it dissolves. Bring the mixture just to the boil, then squeeze out the soaked gelatine and whisk it into the cream. Take the pan off the heat, add the white chocolate and stir until the mixture is smooth. Pour it through a sieve into moulds or small dishes and then refrigerate until set.

For the florentines
Beat the butter with a wooden spoon or an electric mixer, then combine it with the sugar and flour. Chop the nuts quite finely then add them to the butter mixture along with the lemon juice. Stir until well mixed. Place walnut-sized pieces of the mixture on a silicone baking mat, leaving plenty of space between them as they will spread while cooking.

Cook at 180°c for approximately 3 to 4 minutes until lightly browned and the sugar has caramelised. Leave to cool once cooked and then gently remove from the mat to serve with the panna cotta.

RECIPES
& CHEFS

PAUL
PRESTON

Paul Preston

From feeding the British Army to supporting the local community, Paul Preston is always keen to share his extensive experience from a long career in the Navy for the benefit of others.

"The Royal Navy taught me how to cook properly and how to teach other people, which have both been a huge part of my whole career. It also enables you to be a leader and become self-reliant. One of the unique things about the Royal Navy is that you have different jobs every two years. I started cooking in establishments and ships after 8 weeks of training at the cookery school and learnt how to cook in a big kitchen. In those days recipes were rarely used, so we were thrown in at the deep end!

I was a Chief Petty Officer in the catering services by the time I finished my naval career and had also become a cookery instructor twice, at Royal Naval Cookery School Aldershot and HMS Raleigh. That really improved my level of knowledge and because I'd discovered something I really enjoyed, I then took a teaching certificate and completed further qualifications.

For 10 years after my naval career, I was involved with the outside catering service doing dinners and wedding receptions at heritage sites around Portsmouth, which included HMS Victory, Royal Armories and Royal Marines Museum. The travelling I'd done with the Navy was fantastic - as far west as South America, all the way up to the Arctic Circle, and I got to spend two weeks in New York at one point - but there is a lot of separation involved and sometimes that's hard to deal with. You must put down roots somewhere, and I spent eight years away from home due to various roles.

I now work in a defence contract for Sodexo Government and Agencies, which feeds a third of the British Army, as a catering support manager across 60 kitchens. Part of my role is to involve myself in the local community, so I was asked to assess sixth form students' exams at the local Academy here in Tidworth and offer them work experience and apprenticeships. I compete with my young chef recruits at various Hotel, Restaurant and Catering shows across the country including our own Sodexo Salon which I judge. I get a real buzz out of passing on the skills and knowledge I learnt as a catering student. It's my 60th birthday this year and I'm still showing the kids how it's done! That's my biggest passion and a definite career highlight, because I've been able to carry the teaching aspect of my time in the Navy right through my subsequent jobs, and still get real enjoyment from sharing my experience."

Salt Cod with Seafood Cigars

I once had this in Porto and used it for one of my entries at the national cookery championships in London. It's a dish that always reminds me of being on holiday.

Preparation time: 2 hours | Cooking time: 1 hour | Serves 8

Ingredients

For the salt cod
1 cod fillet (400g)
100g sea salt & 1 clove of garlic
2 lemongrass stalks
2 kaffir lime leaves
1 lime, zested and juiced
½ bunch of coriander
½ tsp each Chinese five spice and ground cumin

For the infused oil
4 sprigs each of dill and chervil
400ml extra virgin olive oil
1 lemon, juiced

For the seafood cigars
½ onion, 1 carrot & 1 celery stick
1 sprig each of chervil, dill and tarragon
1 star anise
400ml fish stock
110g mixed seafood
1 lemon, juiced
10g fresh ginger
5g fresh coriander
5g sea salt
190g filo pastry

To serve
300ml red wine jus made with fish stock
4 baby gem lettuces & 20g butter

Method

For the salt cod
Combine all the ingredients except the fish in a bowl. Clean and trim any sinew from the cod fillet. Sprinkle a layer of the salt mixture on a long piece of cling film, lay the cod on top and cover with the rest. Roll up tightly in cling film and press between two heavy trays for 1 hour. Turn the fish over and press for a further 1 hour. Rinse off the salt cure in iced water and pat the cod dry with kitchen paper. Remove the skin and roll tightly in cling film again. Using a sharp knife, portion into eight 50g pieces. Seal each piece into its own small vacuum pack bag.

For the infused oil
Just before serving, poach the cod in a water bath at 50°c for 9 minutes. Meanwhile, combine the fresh herbs, olive oil, lemon juice and a pinch of salt in a saucepan. Warm but do not boil the oil. Remove the cod pieces from their bags and place into the infused olive oil to coat, then place on paper towels to drain.

For the seafood cigars
Finely chop the onion, carrot and celery. Put this mirepoix in a saucepan with the herbs and aromatics, then fill the pan with fish stock. Submerge the seafood in the simmering stock and poach for 6 seconds. Remove and plunge straight into iced water. Transfer the seafood to a food processor with the lemon juice, ginger, coriander and salt. Blitz to a purée, then refrigerate.

Using a ruler and a sharp knife, cut the filo pastry into 10 by 8cm rectangles. Place one piece of pastry onto a board and spread with a 2mm thick layer of the seafood purée. Lay a wooden skewer down the centre and roll the pastry around it. Repeat this process to make seven more cigars. Transfer them to a cling-filmed plate and refrigerate until serving.

To serve
Lay out eight plates with a piece of salt cod on each one. Deep fry the seafood cigars in oil at 180°c until golden. Pull the skewers out and place them on the plates. Remove the outer leaves of the lettuces, reserving the small, pale inners. Gently toss the baby gem hearts in foaming butter. Season with a pinch of salt and divide between the plates. Pour the red wine jus around the cod and lastly, drizzle with some of the infused oil to dress.

Slow Cooked Belly Pork

Served with a stuffed pork fillet, apple soup and garlic purée, this dish is a celebration of classic flavour combinations and well worth the preparation and cooking time for a special occasion! I made this for a competition at Hotelympia London.

Preparation time: 36 hours | Cooking time: 12 hours | Serves 4

Ingredients

100g sea salt
1kg pork belly
500g pork fillet
10g fresh herbs
1 tsp cream
8 slices of Parma ham
2 Bramley apples
2 tbsp caster sugar
100ml white chicken stock
Salt and black pepper
60g butter
6 cloves of garlic
1 tbsp rapeseed oil
4 tbsp double cream
1 tbsp balsamic vinegar
290ml dry white Port

Method

Sprinkle half of the sea salt into a large tray and add the pork belly, skin-side down. Add the rest of the salt on top and rub in well. Cover with cling film and refrigerate for 12 hours.

Preheat the oven to 80°c. Wash and dry the salted pork belly, then wrap in cling film and tin foil. Roast in the oven for 12 hours. Keep the juices for the sauce; you will need about 1.13 litres (2 pints) then place another tray on top of the cooked pork belly and weigh it down. Leave in the fridge for 24 hours. Unwrap the pork belly and cut into portions, then brown on all sides in a frying pan. Place in a warm oven at 150°c until ready to serve.

Trim the pork fillet and place the trimmings in a food processor with the fresh herbs and cream. Blend to make the farce (stuffing). On a large sheet of cling film, lay out the Parma ham with each slice slightly overlapping the next, then put the pork fillet on top. Spread the farce over the pork, then roll up tightly in the ham and tie the cling film at each end to resemble a sausage. Place the stuffed and wrapped pork fillet in a pan of simmering water to cook. When done, it should have a little give rather than being firm, and ideally be slightly pink in the middle. To finish, unwrap the cling film and brown the fillet in a hot pan with some butter.

Place the apples in a saucepan with the sugar, chicken stock and a pinch of salt. Bring to a simmer and cook until soft, then liquidise the mixture and push through a sieve to make a smooth soup. Season to taste with salt and black pepper, stir in a knob of butter and set aside.

Preheat the oven to 160°c. Place the garlic cloves on a large sheet of tin foil, douse with the rapeseed oil and season, then wrap the foil like a parcel and slowly roast the garlic for 1 hour 30 minutes. Peel the cloves and blend to a fine purée in a food processor with the remaining butter (about 50g), double cream and balsamic.

Reduce the pork belly juices in a pan over a medium heat by two thirds. Meanwhile, reduce the white Port until syrupy. Sieve the reduced pork jus into another pan then stir in the Port.

To serve

Lightly cook some seasonal vegetables while you warm all the components of the dish separately, then portion the pork fillet and serve.

Lemon Meringue Tart with Pine Nut Ice Cream

This is a particular favourite of mine; I actually produced this dish in a competition format at the Combined Services cookery competition and won a gold medal. I love lemon as a flavour because it reminds me of summer and my time spent in the Mediterranean.

Preparation time: 1 hour 30 minutes | Cooking time: 1 hour 20 minutes | Serves 8

Ingredients

For the sweet pastry
225g plain flour
110g butter
80g sugar
1 large egg

For the filling
540ml lemon juice
540g caster sugar
540g beaten egg
8g agar agar
700g butter

For the ice cream
485ml full-fat milk
170ml cream
150g caster sugar
70g egg yolk
130g pine nut paste

For the meringue
160g egg white
170g icing sugar

To serve
20g pine nut paste
Sprig of lemon thyme
1 tbsp pine nuts, toasted

Method

For the lemon tart
First, make the pastry. Rub the butter into the flour until the mixture resembles breadcrumbs, then stir in the sugar. Add the egg and enough milk to form a soft dough. Preheat the oven to 160°c and line the base of a 20 to 23cm cake tin with pastry, then chill in the fridge for 30 minutes while you make the filling. Combine the lemon juice, sugar, beaten egg and agar agar in a saucepan over a medium heat. Slowly bring the mixture to a gentle boil, stirring continuously. When it starts to boil, remove from the heat and whisk in the butter gradually. Blind bake the chilled pastry case in the preheated oven 20 minutes or until golden brown, then leave to cool. Pour the lemon filling into the cooled pastry case and leave in the fridge to set.

For the ice cream
Bring the milk and cream to the boil, then take off the heat. Whisk the sugar and yolks together until pale. Pour the warm milk mixture slowly over the yolk mixture while whisking to combine. Whisk in the pine nut paste, then return the mixture to the pan over a low to medium heat. Bring to 80°c while stirring constantly, being careful not to let the mix catch on the base of the pan. Strain, chill and pour into an ice cream machine and churn until you have reached the desired consistency. Freeze.

For the meringue
Preheat the oven to 150°c. Whisk the egg whites with a squeeze of lemon juice until peaks begin to form. Start adding the icing sugar one spoonful at a time and continue to whisk to form stiff peaks. Line two large baking sheets with baking parchment. Spoon half the meringue mixture into a piping bag with a small plain nozzle and pipe 30 x 1 to 2 cm meringues. Use a palette knife to spread the remaining mixture evenly over the second baking sheet 2 or 3 mm thick. Bake both trays in the oven until the meringue is dry and lifts off the parchment easily, about 45 to 60 minutes.

To serve
Cut the lemon tart into portions and place on round plates with a small amount of pine nut paste spread across the plate using a palette knife. Break the sheet of meringue into shards and arrange them around the tart. Carefully caramelise the mini meringues using a blow torch and add them to the plate along with the toasted pine nuts. Finish with a quenelle of the ice cream and sprigs of lemon thyme.

RECIPES & CHEFS
PHIL PRINGLE

Phil Pringle

Having started in the non-military restaurant industry, Phil Pringle moved quickly up the ranks after joining the Navy, came back to civilian life via Newcastle College where he manages the hospitality and catering department, and has since won North East Chef of the Year.

"I made the decision to join the Navy with about six years of industry experience under my belt, knowing that I still wanted to cook but that I also wanted a change of career, to see the world and to serve the country. I also had a lot of family who were ex-forces and a couple of friends in the Navy, so it all seemed to point me in that direction and I was keen to give it a go. Within two years of joining in 1999 I was promoted to Leading Hand in the kitchen, and the year after that I began teaching at the Royal Navy Cookery School in Plymouth.

I represented the Navy in a variety of national competitions including Hotelympia during the first year of my basic training, and Salon Culinaire. In 2005, I won Royal Navy Senior Chef of the Year and was part of a team that cooked for the Queen, amidst deployments and world tours on the Ocean and Bulwark. In 2008 I was made Petty Officer, leading the catering operations on both those ships, as well as the Royal Navy Culinary Arts Team Captain. There's absolutely no doubt I would have stayed in the Navy for my full 22 years, but in 2011 I was medically discharged.

Although gutted that I couldn't continue my naval career, the first thing I thought of was getting back into teaching cookery, and immediately found employment at Newcastle College, the school I'd been to growing up. Today I manage the hospitality and catering department having worked my way up over the years. We train chefs from apprentice level to full-time students and also offer a degree in Culinary Arts. I think teaching suits me because I love talking about food, and a key point in my career was the time I was fortunate enough to become a chef instructor at the Royal Navy Cookery School. There's nothing better than watching students who struggle become confident under your guidance, and I fell in love with passing on my skills.

For me, being stretched and challenged is the best way to improve so I encourage our students to enter competitions and get hands-on experience like I did. The drive to constantly evolve my knowledge, palate and technical skills hasn't left me, and the travelling I've done has enabled me to see what other chefs are doing everywhere I go. In 2018, I won North East Chef of the Year by creating and cooking the menu I've shared for this book. Joining the Navy was a huge factor in getting to where I am now, so it's great to give back a little with these special recipes."

Scallops with Greens, Textures of Jerusalem Artichoke and Beurre Blanc

This is a simple but very effective dish which has a lot of flavour and texture. You can get your fishmonger to shell the scallops; hand-dived are the best. Use Jerusalem artichokes from about October to March, or other vegetables such as parsnip or celeriac if they are unavailable.

Preparation time: 1 hour | Cooking time: 1 hour 30 minutes | Serves 4

Ingredients

12 scallops with roe
25g butter, softened
1 tsp curry powder
Pinch of salt, to taste (no more than 2-3g)

For the artichoke purée
200g Jerusalem artichokes
20ml double cream

For the artichoke crisps
1 Jerusalem artichoke
Vegetable oil, for deep frying

For the butter sauce
½ banana shallot, finely diced
30ml white wine vinegar
20ml double cream
100g cold butter, diced
Salt and ground white pepper
A few chives, finely chopped

For the greens
20g butter
100g wild garlic
100g baby spinach

Method

First, mix the curry powder and salt into the softened butter. Lightly dust the scallops with salt and pepper, just enough to liberally cover each side, then sear them in a hot pan with a little oil. Do not move or shake the pan, leave them for about 1 minute, then turn the scallops over. The cooked side should now be golden brown. Leave for another minute then add a teaspoon of the curried butter. Turn the scallops over again after 30 seconds and baste with the frothing butter, then place them on kitchen paper to rest for 10-20 seconds before serving. I also like to dry the scallop roe out in the oven, either until cooked and then dice it, or dried completely and then blended to a powder, to be added to the butter sauce for maximum flavour.

For the artichoke purée

Peel and dice the artichokes, then put the prepared veg into a saucepan with 1 litre of water and a pinch of salt. Bring to the boil and leave to simmer for 15 to 20 minutes until the artichokes are soft, then drain thoroughly (reserving some of the cooking water) and transfer to a blender. Add the double cream and a little of the cooking water, then blend until smooth. Check the seasoning then push through a fine sieve.

For the artichoke crisps

Peel the artichoke then slice on a mandoline, or very thinly using a sharp knife. Deep fry the slices at 175°c until they start to colour, then drain and cool on paper towels.

For the butter sauce

Sweat the shallot with a little of the butter in a hot pan until soft, but do not let it colour. Add the white wine vinegar and reduce the volume of liquid until a syrupy consistency is achieved. Stir in the double cream, then bring to the boil and reduce the volume of liquid by half. Take the pan off direct heat and gradually add the cold cubed butter while stirring constantly. Taste the sauce and season it accordingly with salt and ground white pepper. Strain the sauce through a fine sieve, fold in the chopped chives and cooked scallop roe, then serve immediately.

For the greens

Bring 300ml of water and the butter to the boil in a wide saucepan, then add a pinch of salt. Drop the wild garlic and spinach into the pan and stir for 40 to 50 seconds. Drain in a colander then place on paper towels for 20 seconds to remove the excess liquid. Squeeze out the remaining moisture and serve immediately.

Trio of Pork

This dish uses three different textures of pork: the expensive tenderloin (or fillet), the cheaper offal, and the crackling. I like to serve this with fondant potato, roasted shallots and carrots. You can use ready-made stock for convenience, although the flavour of the finished sauce may not be as rich.

Preparation time: 2 hours | Cooking time: 10-12 hours | Serves 4

Ingredients

1 pork tenderloin
1 piece of dry pork rind
Vegetable oil

For the veal stock

1kg veal bones
1 pig's trotter & 1 ham hock
200g chopped celery, carrot and onions
1 bulb of garlic

For the jus lié

1 onion and carrot, chopped
2 sticks of celery, chopped
½ bulb of garlic, chopped
120ml madeira
1 heaped tbsp tomato purée
2 litres veal stock
2 sprigs of thyme
1 bay leaf & 10g parsley stalks
50g fresh morels, washed & dried
1 tbsp double cream
10g cold butter (optional)

For the offal faggot

4 Savoy cabbage leaves
80g pork liver, heart & kidney
80g dry breadcrumbs
1 tsp chopped parsley & thyme
1 tsp Dijon mustard
1 egg, beaten
Salt and black pepper

Method

For the veal stock

Brown off the bones, trotter and ham hock in a large pan. Drain off any liquid, then do the same with the chopped vegetables and garlic. Combine them all in a stock pot then fill it to the top with 2 to 3 litres of cold water. Bring to the boil, skim any froth off the surface, then simmer the stock for 8 to 10 hours. Strain and cool before using.

For the jus lié

Heat a tablespoon of vegetable oil in a large pan, then sauté the vegetables until browned. Add the madeira. This can be flamed to burn off the alcohol or left to reduce to a syrup. Add the tomato purée and stir for 2 minutes. Add the stock and herbs. Bring to the boil then simmer for 1 hour. Strain the liquid through a sieve into a clean pan, then reduce for an hour. It should coat the back of a metal spoon. 2 minutes before serving the dish, add the morels to the sauce and bring it to the boil. Stir the cream in thoroughly and do not let it boil (it will split). If desired, whisk in the butter to increase the flavour and add shine to the sauce.

For the offal faggot

Devein and blanch the Savoy cabbage leaves in boiling salted water for 3 to 4 minutes, then rinse under cold water and drain. Pat dry with kitchen paper. Chop the offal and combine it with the remaining ingredients, seasoning the mixture with salt and pepper to taste. Place a square of cling film on the worktop and lay a cabbage leaf in the centre. Place a spoonful of the offal mixture into the centre of the leaf and wrap tightly, using the cling film to make a ball. Repeat with the remaining cabbage and filling, then rest the faggots in the fridge. Cook in simmering stock or water for 15 to 20 minutes, then unwrap the cling film, drain and serve immediately.

For the pork crackling

Scrape the rind clean of fat, cut into strips and coat these lightly with olive oil, then season with salt and pepper. Bake in the oven between sheets of greaseproof paper and two heavy trays at 180°c for 30 minutes.

For the pork tenderloin

Sear the tenderloin in a very hot pan with a tablespoon of vegetable oil, turning it every 6 to 8 seconds. When thoroughly sealed, remove the tenderloin and pat dry with kitchen roll. I like to brush a little Dijon mustard over the whole fillet, then roll it in blitzed dried wild mushrooms. Place the tenderloin on a tray and bake in the hot oven for 9 to 10 minutes, then leave to rest for 5 to 6 minutes before carving and serving.

Petit Antoine (A Chocolatier's Dream)

This is a crowd pleaser and very simple to make; the different elements take a little time and patience but can all be made in advance. You can buy chocolate lids to sit on top of the dessert if you like, or make your own with tempered chocolate cut to size.

Preparation time: 2 hours | Cooking time: 25 minutes | Serves 4

Ingredients

For the almond cocoa streusel

150g Demerara sugar
150g ground almonds
115g plain flour
25g cocoa powder
Pinch of salt & 150g butter, diced

For the chocolate crumble

160g chocolate
30g sunflower oil
130g chocolate pearls

For the dark chocolate mousse

3 egg yolks
30g caster sugar
200g dark chocolate
300g whipping cream

For the coffee cream

200ml double cream
1 heaped tbsp icing sugar
1 capful coffee liqueur

For the mango coulis

1 whole ripe mango
300ml pre-made mango coulis
1 tbsp caster sugar

For the salted popcorn

7g vegetable oil
20g popcorn kernels
10g caster sugar

Method

For the almond cocoa streusel

Combine the dry ingredients, then using your fingers or a food processor, rub the diced butter into the almond mixture to a breadcrumb texture. Pour the streusel onto a baking tray and bake in the oven at 170°c for 10 minutes, then leave to cool.

For the chocolate crumble

Melt the chocolate with the oil making sure it gets no hotter than 40°c. Combine it with 240g of the cooled streusel, the pearls and a pinch of salt, to taste. Mix everything together then decant into moulds or ramekins to a depth of 0.5cm or less. Place in the fridge to set.

For the dark chocolate mousse

Whisk the egg yolks and sugar together over a bowl of pan of hot water to make a sabayon. Separately, melt the chocolate (making sure it gets no hotter than 45°c) and whip the cream to soft peak stage. Mix half of the whipped cream into the melted chocolate, then add the sabayon. Fold in the rest of the cream until combined but be careful not to overwork the mousse and lose the air. Pipe or spoon the mousse onto the set crumble base in the moulds, then smooth the surface with a palette knife and place back in the fridge to set.

For the coffee cream

Whip the cream with the icing sugar and coffee liqueur using a balloon whisk until it forms soft peaks. Pipe the coffee cream into little peaks on top of the set mousse.

For the mango coulis

Peel and chop the mango, place into a saucepan, cover with the pre-made mango coulis, then add the sugar and a little water to help the fruit cook. Bring to the boil and simmer for 15 minutes. Blend then strain through a fine sieve. Leave to cool, then place into the fridge. Drizzle around the plated petit antoine before serving.

For the salted popcorn

Gently heat the oil in a saucepan, then stir in the popcorn kernels until coated. Add the sugar and salt to taste, stir again, then cover with a lid and shake while the popcorn cooks. Once all the popping has stopped, tip the popcorn onto a tray and leave to cool before serving.

RECIPES
& CHEFS

RYAN ASHALL

Ryan Ashall

From a chance encounter with cooking at his first part-time job, Ryan Ashall's culinary career has been marked by dedication and drive, and attributes his success to the great teams he has worked with and the support of his family.

"My interest in cooking began while I was working part-time at a restaurant. They were short staffed and asked if I could help out, and I just got the buzz for it immediately. This is where my passion for food began, and it was my Nan who suggested I join the Navy. By the time I started training at HMS Raleigh at the age of 18, I was already set on being a chef.

Cooking was never something I was naturally gifted at, and I struggled to find my way in a military lifestyle at first. I started off as a junior chef in the veg section at CTC Lympstone, the marine barracks, but soon got the opportunity to be more artistic with my cooking when I joined the HMS Campbeltown, my first ship. It had a wardroom galley which gave us more space and flexibility to create fine dining, so I was able to experiment with combining flavours, plating food, and adding my own personal touch to the dishes.

I had always said that I would leave the Navy after four years, then I said the same thing again after eight years, then twelve. Short term goals very much turned into a long term love of the Navy and in 2020, I was awarded my Long Service medal by the commodore to celebrate 15 years in service. I've been very blessed in my career, and I'm always trying to keep it fresh and push the boundaries with my cooking.

While on board HMS Ocean, I had the opportunity to cook for the Queen and was asked to be head chef for that event. I worked with a select team of chefs to design the menu and everything we achieved, we achieved together. I'm only as good as my team, especially where my family is concerned. My wife, Kelly, and the kids have supported me and allowed me to be selfish at times to reach my goals, so my achievements are absolutely theirs as much as mine.

Another rewarding experience I've had as a Naval rating outside of cooking was going to the Caribbean to help with disaster relief. It feels great to be able to make a difference for people in very hard circumstances. I'm always thinking about how I can help the next generation and keep everything moving forward."

HMS Ocean Gin and Tonic
Cured Pollock

I used a specially made gin for the decommissioning, but you can use any of your favourites in this recipe. Hendricks gin works well in this combination of flavours. The cured fish is served with compressed and powdered cucumber, dill oil, crème fraîche and a pumpernickel crumb.

Preparation time: 12 hours | Cooking time: 35-40 minutes | Serves 8

Ingredients

For the cured fish
50g each fine table salt and
caster sugar
25g lemon zest
75ml gin and 25ml tonic
1kg pollock

For the pumpernickel crumb
200g strong wholemeal flour
75g rye flour
30g cornmeal
20g muscovado sugar
2 tbsp instant yeast
1 tsp salt
230ml warm milk
30g molasses sugar
15ml vegetable oil

For the cucumber garnishes
1 cucumber
½ tsp salt
1 tbsp honey
3 tbsp rapeseed oil

For the dill garnishes
120ml olive oil
60g fresh dill
400g crème fraîche
Sea salt and black peppercorns

Method

For the cured fish
Mix all the ingredients except the pollock together. Line a large dish with cling film and cover it with half the salt cure, lay the pollock fillet on top and cover it with the remaining cure. Cover completely with cling film and leave to cure for a minimum of 8 hours in the fridge. After this time, the fish will be firm and have a salty flavour. Wash the cure off thoroughly, drain and dry the fish with kitchen paper.

Preheat the oven to 150°c or 130°c fan. Put the fish in a roasting tin, drizzle with some oil and cover with tin foil. Cook the fish in the preheated oven for 10 minutes, then leave to cool before wrapping in cling film and refrigerating. Cut the cured and chilled fish into 0.5cm slices to serve.

For the pumpernickel crumb
Combine the flours, cornmeal, muscovado sugar, yeast and salt in a large bowl. Pour the milk, molasses sugar and oil into the centre and begin to mix, using your hands when it starts to form a dough. Knead for 10 to 15 minutes until the dough is smooth and stretchy, place the dough in a lightly oiled bowl and leave to rise for 30 minutes.

Knock back the dough and shape it into a large oval. Place on a baking tray and cover with a damp tea towel. Leave to prove again for 1 hour. Meanwhile, preheat the oven to 190°c or 180°c fan. Bake the bread for 30 minutes, covering the top with foil for the last 10 minutes to prevent it from going too brown. Cool on a wire rack.

Once cooled, slice your bread and leave to go slightly stale before blitzing the slices in a food processor to make the crumb.

For the cucumber garnishes
Peel and deseed the cucumber, saving the skin. Dry the cucumber skin in a cool oven, then grind to a powder. Mix the salt, honey and oil together in a vacuum pack bag. Cut the prepared cucumber into 1cm cubes and add these to the dressing in the bag before sealing to compress.

For the dill garnishes
Put the olive oil and 40g of the dill into a food processor. Blitz until there are green speckles of dill throughout the oil. Whisk the crème fraîche to soft peaks, then finely chop and fold in the remaining dill. Season with salt and pepper, then serve your garnishes with the slices of cured pollock.

Roasted Loin of Dartmoor Venison

I like to serve this autumnal dish with boulangère potatoes, celeriac purée and a venison jus, garnished with pan-roasted wild mushrooms and parsnip crisps.

Preparation time: 30 minutes | Cooking time: 1 hour | Serves 8

Ingredients

1.5kg venison loin
Olive oil and seasoning

For the venison jus

4 shallots, peeled and sliced
1 clove of garlic, peeled
100ml each red wine vinegar and red wine
400ml Port
2 litres veal stock
1 litre chicken stock
1 bay leaf and 1 sprig of thyme
1 heaped tbsp tomato purée
700g venison bones, chopped and roasted

For the boulangère potatoes

2 medium-size onions, peeled & sliced
1.5 kg Desirée or Maris Piper potatoes, peeled & sliced
10g fresh rosemary
275ml vegetable stock
150ml milk & 40g butter

For the celeriac purée

750g celeriac, peeled
375ml milk
150ml thickened cream
50g shallots, coarsely chopped
20g butter & 1 tsp fine sea salt

For the garnishes

100g Clamshell mushrooms
3 parsnips, peeled

Method

First, trim the venison loin of any fat and wipe clean with kitchen paper. Rub with olive oil, season with salt and black pepper, then set aside.

For the venison jus

Sweat the shallots and garlic in olive oil. Add the vinegar and reduce to a glaze, then repeat with the other alcohols. Add the remaining ingredients and reduce to your preferred consistency. Strain the sauce through a muslin and season. Keep warm.

For the boulangère potatoes

Butter an ovenproof dish measuring 28 by 20 by 5cm. Brown the onions in a frying pan with some olive oil. Layer the potatoes and onions in the dish, scatter over some rosemary and seasoning, then firmly press down each layer. Finish with a layer of potatoes that slightly overlap. Combine the stock and milk, pour over the potatoes, season the top layer, then put flecks of butter all over the potatoes. Place the dish on the highest shelf of the oven to cook at 180°c for 1 hour, until the top is crisp and golden and the centre is creamy and tender.

For the celeriac purée

Combine all the ingredients in a saucepan and bring to a simmer. Reduce the heat and simmer gently, stirring occasionally, for 35 minutes. The celeriac should be tender enough to mash. Working in batches using a slotted spoon, transfer the celeriac and shallots to a blender and blend until smooth, adding enough of the cooking liquid to form a very thick and creamy smooth purée. Transfer to a serving bowl.

For the garnishes

Heat some olive oil in a frying pan and lightly cook the mushrooms until slightly wilted. Add a knob of butter and toss the mushrooms until coated, then take off the heat. Peel thick ribbons from the parsnips, deep fry these in hot oil until golden brown, then pat dry to remove any excess oil. Season the crisps with sea salt.

To serve

Preheat the oven to 180°c and heat some vegetable oil in an ovenproof frying pan. Sear the venison loin on all sides until dark brown, then roast for 10 to 12 minutes for medium rare. Remove it from the oven, cover with foil and rest for 10 minutes. Trim off both ends, then slice into 4cm portions and serve with the rest of the dish.

White Chocolate and Vanilla Panna Cotta with Passionfruit

This recipe requires some specialist equipment: silicone moulds for the panna cotta, a sugar thermometer for the passionfruit crumb, and a transfer sheet to create patterns on the tempered chocolate shard. I used Silikomart No.9 Midi Buche moulds, but you can use any mould or glass you have available.

Preparation time: 30 minutes, plus 1-2 hours setting | Cooking time: 30 minutes | Serves 8

Ingredients

For the panna cotta
2 vanilla pods, halved
900ml double cream
225ml milk
115g caster sugar
115g white chocolate
4 gelatine leaves

For the passionfruit gel
125ml passionfruit purée
55g caster sugar
80ml water
4 gelatine leaves

For the passionfruit crumb
200g caster sugar
4 tbsp water
140g Callebaut white chocolate drops
50g freeze-dried passionfruit

For the passionfruit coulis
5 passionfruit, halved
125g caster sugar

For the chocolate shards
150g Callebaut dark chocolate, tempered

Method

For the panna cotta
Scrape the vanilla seeds into a large pan with the cream, milk and sugar in. Gently bring to a simmer, then add the chocolate and stir until melted. Soak the gelatine in 2 tablespoons of cold water, then add to the pan and stir until fully incorporated. Fill your moulds with the panna cotta mixture to just below the halfway point. Place in the fridge for 1 to 2 hours, or until set.

For the passionfruit gel
Do not start this process until the panna cotta is almost set. Combine the passionfruit purée, sugar and water in a small saucepan. Cook while stirring over a low heat for 3 minutes, or until the sugar has dissolved. Soak the gelatine in 2 tablespoons of cold water, then add to the pan and stir until fully incorporated. Transfer the mixture to a jug and set aside to cool. Before it has fully set, pour it over the set panna cotta mixture in the moulds, filling them almost to the top. Once both the layers are fully set you will need to gently turn the layered panna cottas out of the moulds.

For the passionfruit crumb
Heat the sugar and water in a saucepan. Once it reaches 130°c, take the pan off the heat and add the white chocolate. Whisk until the mixture has a sandy texture. If you like, pulse in a food processor to get a finer consistency. Pulse the freeze-dried passionfruit to the same texture as your chocolate crumb, then mix together.

For the passionfruit coulis
Scoop all the passionfruit pulp and seeds into a saucepan, add the sugar and bring to the boil over a medium heat. Simmer for 4 to 5 minutes. Strain the mixture to get a smooth liquid. Add a few of the black seeds back in for visual effect. Leave the coulis in the fridge to cool.

For the chocolate shards
Spread the tempered chocolate onto your patterned transfer sheet thinly and evenly, then place in the fridge to set, for 20 to 30 minutes. Gently peel off the set chocolate sheet, which should be shiny and patterned, lay it on a flat surface and use a hot knife to gently cut out your desired shapes. Take care as the chocolate will be delicate. Serve the layered panna cotta with the crumb, coulis and chocolate shards.

RECIPES
& CHEFS
RYAN
HOPPER

Ryan Hopper

Ryan Hopper left the Royal Navy as a Petty Officer with national and international titles under his belt. He was the Naval Services Culinary Arts Team and Combined Services Culinary Arts Team captain, the latter being a great honour, being the only member of the Navy as part of the team.

"Being a chef was never part of my plan. In fact, neither was being in the Royal Navy. On leaving school I had always planned to go to uni and study Graphic Design. However, after a uni day at the age of 15, I realised immediately that it wasn't for me. Instead, I got a part-time job in a butcher's, and absolutely loved it – the face-to-face engagement, the busy atmosphere, learning about food.

Everything changed when a friend of mine joined the Royal Navy and inspired me and six other mates to give it a go. We made a £50 bet – we would all join and see who could last the longest. That was in 1987 and I think I am officially the winner. I've not claimed that £50 yet, though!

I joined as a cook, went through my training and joined my first warship. It was during my first deployment to the West Indies where I felt myself really start to fall in love with life as a chef in the Royal Navy. I found it all fascinating and there was just so much to learn. I discovered a thirst for knowledge, from the science behind food to the history of cooking. It triggered my passion for the culinary world and paved the way for me to start competing.

My first competition was in 1992 and I came away with a gold medal in my first event. The buzz was incredible. I joined the Cookery School at HMS Raleigh as an instructor, and it was from this point that I really stepped into competitions. I became a member of the Combined Services Culinary Arts Team in 2006, was voted captain in 2008 and headed the team for the next 3 years. From winning double gold medals at the Culinary Olympics to finishing fourth in the world in the Culinary World Cup, there were so many highlights.

After 24 years in the Royal Navy I moved to Compass Group UK in 2013 and I am now a Regional Executive Chef at ESS Defence. I was honoured to be named Public Sector Chef of the Year at the Craft Guild of Chefs Awards in 2019 – another amazing career highlight. I am currently enjoying the mentoring side of my role, guiding young chefs to achieve the best they can."

Mackerel and Root Veg

This delicate starter comprises Earl Grey tea-smoked Cornish mackerel, warm pickled root vegetables, beetroot purée, oyster emulsion, crispy oysters and pea shoots.

Preparation time: 1 hour | Cooking time: 1 hour | Serves 4

Ingredients

For the crispy oysters and emulsion
8 fresh oysters

1 egg yolk

30ml rapeseed oil

1 litre vegetable oil

100g plain flour

100ml sparkling water, chilled

For the beetroot purée
300g beetroot

For the golden beetroot
200g golden beets

For the pickled root veg
4 radishes & 300g carrots

1 fennel bulb

300g daikon

150g candy-striped beetroot

500ml cider vinegar

80g caster sugar

10g yellow mustard seeds

10g black peppercorns

5 cloves & 2 star anise

For the mackerel
50g Earl Grey loose tea leaves

2 whole Cornish mackerel, filleted and pin-boned

To garnish
50g pea shoots

Method

For the oysters and emulsion
Shuck the oysters, retaining any liquor for use in the emulsion. Pass the liquor through a fine sieve to remove any impurities. Add the yolk to a clean pan. Gently whisk and slowly pour in the oyster liquor. Once combined, drizzle in the rapeseed oil whilst whisking, achieving a silky texture.

For the beetroot purée, golden beetroot and pickled root veg
Cook the beetroot separately by adding them to two pans, covering with water and simmering until tender. Peel all the beets, then purée the red and dice the golden into 1cm cubes. Thinly slice the radishes and fennel. Peel the carrots, daikon and candy-striped beetroots. Cut the carrot into thin strips. Slice the candy-striped beetroots into 1.5mm discs, then, using a 3cm round cutter, create discs. Dice the daikon into 2.5mm cubes. Combine 450ml of the vinegar with the sugar, mustard seeds, peppercorns, cloves and star anise in a pan. Bring to a simmer and then add all the prepared vegetables. Remove from the heat and allow to cool.

For the mackerel
Put the tea leaves in a dry frying pan, cover with foil and gently heat. Pierce the foil multiple times and lay the mackerel on top. When smoke appears, cover with a lid. Heat for roughly 5 minutes, then remove from the heat. Leave covered until required.

For the oysters
Place the vegetable oil into a small handled pan so that it is between one-third and one-half full. Heat. Mix the flour and chilled sparkling water together to create a loose batter. Test the oil by sticking the end of a wooden spoon into the oil. If you see bubbles form and float up, your oil is ready for frying. If it is bubbling hard, the oil is too hot so let it cool. Once correct, dip the oyster into the batter and add to the oil. Cook until lightly golden. Remove with a slotted spoon and drain on kitchen paper.

To serve
Lightly warm the beet purée and place a spoonful to one side of each plate. Using the spoon, drag it across the plate. Drain the warm pickled vegetables. Dress across the purée, retaining the candy-striped beets. Check that the mackerel is cooked through (use a fork to gently flake one end – if it parts easily then the fillet is cooked). Place the fillet across the dressed vegetables. Add the crispy oyster and dot the emulsion around the vegetables. Finally, garnish with the pea shoots, candy-striped beets and golden beets, and serve.

Beef and Asparagus

This classic West Country Beef Wellington is served with fondant potato, butternut purée, griddled English asparagus and Parmesan, sautéed girolles and jus.

Preparation time: 1 hour | Cooking time: 3 hours | Serves 4

Ingredients

For the beef wellington
1kg ruby red beef fillet
300g chestnut mushrooms, finely diced
100g unsalted butter
300g baby spinach
500g ready-rolled puff pastry
3 egg yolks, lightly beaten
Plain flour, for dusting

For the jus
200g carrots, roughly chopped
200g onions, roughly chopped
2 pig's trotters

For the butternut purée
500g butternut squash, peeled, deseeded and roughly diced
50ml double cream

For the fondant potatoes
4 baking potatoes
50g unsalted butter

For the asparagus and girolles
300g fine asparagus, trimmed
50g unsalted butter
250g Perigord girolles, halved or quartered

To serve
50g Parmesan, finely grated

Method

For the beef wellington and jus
Trim all sinew and fat and shape the fillet to a 10cm cylinder. Discard all sinew and fat. Retain the trimmings for the stock. Roll into a tight cylinder in cling film and chill. Gently fry the carrots and onions. Add the meat trimmings and fry for 5 minutes, lightly browning. Add to a pot with the pig's trotters and 2 litres of water. Bring to the boil and then reduce to a simmer, skimming off any scum. Simmer for 1.5 hours, skimming throughout. Meanwhile, sauté the diced mushrooms in 50g of the butter. Remove from the pan and allow to cool. Add the spinach to the same pan and gently dry fry. Remove and cool. Remove the fillet from the clingfilm. Add the remaining 50g butter to a frying pan and gently fry, rolling and basting, until light golden. Let cool.

For the butternut purée and fondant potatoes
Gently boil the butternut squash. When cooked, drain, purée and return to the pot. Add the cream and cool. Preheat the oven to 180°c. Shape the potatoes into a rectangles. Add the butter to a pan and gently colour the top side of the potatoes. Add to an ovenproof dish with enough beef stock to reach halfway up the potatoes. Cover and bake for 1 hour until cooked through, then uncover to finish colouring.

For the beef wellington and jus
Strain the rest of the stock through a fine sieve and return to the heat. Reduce until the jus coats the back of a spoon. Keep warm. Preheat the oven to 200°c. Lay the pastry out on a flour-dusted surface. Spread the cooled spinach out to 3cm from the edge. Squeeze any excess liquid from the mushrooms and then lay onto the spinach. Add the fillet to the centre, ensuring the pastry will encompass it all. Egg wash one side of the pastry and roll up. Lay the wellington onto a lightly greased baking sheet with the seal on the base. Lightly score the pastry top and glaze with egg yolk. Cook for 14 minutes. Rest on a wire rack over the baking tray.

For the asparagus and girolles
Add the butter to a pan and gently cook the asparagus. Keep warm on kitchen paper. Add the girolles to the same pan and gently fry until cooked.

To serve
Warm the butternut purée and place a spoonful at 2 o'clock on the plate, dragging into the centre. Slice the end from the wellington to reveal the core, then cut a 3-4cm thick slice. Plate the dish as shown opposite. Add the jus and serve.

Yoghurt and Rhubarb

Baked Trewithen yoghurt served with roasted and poached rhubarb, confit blood orange
and sweet cicely.

Preparation time: 30 minutes | Cooking time: 30 minutes | Serves 4

Ingredients

For the baked yoghurt
100g condensed milk
100g double cream
110g Trewithen yoghurt or
Greek yoghurt
Seeds of 1 vanilla pod

For the roasted rhubarb
200g rhubarb
20g caster sugar
2 oranges, zested (use the juice
for the citrus Chantilly)

For the confit blood orange
30g caster sugar
2 blood oranges

For the citrus Chantilly
100ml double cream
10g icing sugar
2 oranges, juiced

To serve
50g sweet cicely

Method

For the baked yoghurt
Preheat the oven to 150°c and the water bath to a temperature of 65°c. Combine the condensed milk, double cream, yoghurt and vanilla seeds in a large bowl. Mix well, then strain through a fine chinois. Divide the yoghurt mixture between your chosen serving dishes (ovenproof pots or ramekins – though I prefer a whisky glass), placing about 70g in each. Arrange the pots inside a deep tray (you may find it easier to do this before adding the yoghurt mixture), then fill the tray with warm water to come one-quarter of the way up the pots, creating a bain-marie. Stretch a layer of cling film over the tray and place in the oven. Cook until the yoghurt is set; this should take about 12 minutes. Once cooked, remove the cling film and leave to cool to room temperature, then chill in the fridge until needed.

For the roasted rhubarb
Preheat the oven to 175°c. Cut the rhubarb into batons. Toss in the sugar and orange zest, and place into an ovenproof dish. Roast for 6-8 minutes and allow to cool. Remove the roasted batons and reserve the juice.

For the confit blood orange
Peel the blood oranges. Separate the flesh into segments and set aside. Remove the pith and cut the peel into fine strips. Bring a saucepan of water to the boil. Submerge the sliced peel in the water, then immediately refresh in a bowl of iced water. Blanch the peel in this way twice more, using fresh water each time. Place the sugar and 50ml of water in a small saucepan over a low heat. When the sugar has completely dissolved and the mixture is gently simmering, add the orange segments and the blanched peel and poach until translucent. Allow to cool.

For the citrus Chantilly
Place the double cream, icing sugar and orange juice in a bowl, and mix with a whisk until the cream forms soft peaks. Spoon into a piping bag and store in the fridge.

To serve
Spoon some of the rhubarb liquid onto each set yoghurt pot and dot with the citrus Chantilly. Top with the blood orange segments and rhubarb pieces, and finish with a garnish of poached orange peel and sweet cicely.

RECIPES
&
CHEFS
SCOTT
FURBER

Scott Furber

With a career in the Royal Navy spanning 16 years and his own chocolate business, Scott Furber is an award-winning chef with an impressive array of talents.

"I joined the Royal Navy in 2005. After completing my training I Joined HMS Nelson in Portsmouth, and it was once I was working on-board that I felt I began to flourish as a chef. I loved catering for grand dinner parties and fine dining was where my passion for cooking really took hold.

My career has taken me all over the world and it has given me such breadth of experience as a chef. From feeding hundreds of hungry sailors to preparing exquisite dinner parties for Royalty, I fell in love with cooking in all its many variations. I began endlessly researching, always buying new cookbooks and pushing myself to learn about food. I entered competitions and began to develop a love for chocolate work, an interest which was self-taught and has since progressed into my own chocolate business, Inspiration of Chocolate.

In 2014 I joined Retinue Support Pool (RSP) in Portsmouth; a pool of Leading Chefs who look after and cook for all the Admiralty within the Portsmouth Dockyard Area. Feeding Royalty and Heads of States on numerous occasions led to my promotion to Petty Officer in 2016, where I took over the role as Head Chef. This role opened my eyes to different cuisines and methods of cooking. A highlight for me was working alongside world famous chef Anton Edelmann (Head Chef of the Savoy 1982-2003), cooking and serving the Trafalgar Night Dinner on board HMS VICTORY in Admiral Lord Nelson's Great Cabin.

I joined HMS DUNCAN in 2017, where I led a team of 10 chefs. the Royal Navy is famously very traditional in its ways of cooking, and I was passionate about trying to change the way food was perceived on board. For example, the tradition to have fish on Friday had become synonymous with battered fish and chips, so I experimented with dishes such as salmon and crushed new potatoes. I enjoyed not only putting fresh ideas on the menu, but also championing healthier options. My efforts were rewarded when I won Armed Forces Caterer of the Year in 2018.

After a stint teaching at the cookery school at Worthy Down, I was promoted to Chief Petty Officer in 2021 and joined the Royal Navy's biggest Warship HMS PRINCE OF WALES. Here, I am currently in charge of delivery of food to up to 1600 people over 4 different galleys. I love the variation in my role – from overseeing the cooking for hundreds of people every day to putting together impressive dinner parties for Royal guests. It's a fine balance of logistics and creativity, skills which I have had the opportunity to learn in the Royal Navy."

Salmon and Pickled Lemon Tartare

The salmon and pickled lemon tartare is served with pickled beetroot, soy-cured quail's egg yolk, curried granola with goat's cheese mousse and beetroot gel. The pickled lemon needs to be made 48 hours in advance.

Preparation time: 2 hours, plus 48 hours pickling | Cooking time: 1 hour | Serves 4

Ingredients

For the tartare
190ml white wine vinegar
95g caster sugar & 2 lemons
400g salmon side, skinned and de-boned
1 gherkin, salt and pepper
Micro lemon balm, to garnish

For the pickled beetroot
200ml apple vinegar
100g caster sugar
1 tsp juniper berries
1 tsp mustard seeds
3 star anise
1 tsp pink peppercorns
2 large red beetroots

For the curried granola
85g porridge oats
120ml rapeseed oil
50g wild rice
30g chopped pistachio nuts
30g Rice Krispies & 170g honey
25g madras curry powder

For the goat's cheese mousse
150g goat's cheese
100ml double cream

For the beetroot gel
500ml beetroot juice
Ultratex, as needed

For the quail's egg yolk
8 quail's eggs & 120ml soy sauce

Method

For the salmon and pickled lemon tartare
Bring the vinegar, sugar and 250ml of water to the boil. Dissolve and cool. Thinly slice the lemons, then finely dice. Add to the cooled pickling liquid and allow to pickle for up to 48 hours in the fridge. Strain the liquid and place the lemon into a separate dish in the fridge. Finely dice the salmon and gherkin, cover and place in the fridge.

For the pickled beetroot and curried granola
Bring the vinegar, sugar and 200ml of water to the boil. Stir to dissolve and add the juniper berries, mustard seeds, star anise and peppercorns. Once boiled, remove from the heat and cool. Strain the liquid and remove the spices. Retain the liquid. Thinly slice the beetroot using a mandoline. Use a 3cm circle cutter to cut out about 30 discs. Add them to the cooled liquid and pickle for 8 hours. Preheat the oven to 90°c. Mix the oats with 3 tablespoons of oil. Place on a lined baking tray and bake for 30 minutes. Cool. Increase the oven to 135°c. Add half a teaspoon of oil to a frying pan and set over a high heat until it starts to smoke. Pour half of the rice into the hot oil and stir constantly for 20 seconds; the rice will puff up and be light brown. Transfer onto kitchen roll and repeat with the rest of the rice. Combine the oats with the puffed rice, pistachios and Rice Krispies. In a small pan combine the remaining 60ml of oil, the honey, curry powder and 1 tablespoon of water. Bring to the boil, then pour over the dry ingredients. Mix well. Transfer to a lined baking tray and bake for 8 minutes. Stir, then return to the oven for 8 minutes. Allow to cool, then break into pieces.

For the goat's cheese mousse, beetroot gel and soy-cured quail's egg yolk
Put the goat's cheese and half the cream into a food processor, pulsing until incorporated. Add more cream until you have a smooth consistency. Transfer to a piping bag. Place the beetroot juice into a tall-sided pan over a high heat. Let it boil and reduce by half. Add Ultratex, 1 tablespoon at a time, and blitz with a hand blender until gel-like. Transfer to a piping bag. Separate the egg yolks from the whites. Place the yolks into a bowl, pour the soy onto them and let them sit for 10 minutes.

To serve
Combine the pickled lemon, gherkin and salmon, and season. Use a 7cm circle cutter to form into rounds on plates, smoothing the tops flat. Layer 6 beetroot discs on top of each, overlapping them but leaving a little hole in the centre. Pipe 3 blobs of goat's cheese mousse around the salmon, then fill in the gaps with curried granola. Pipe 5 dots of beetroot gel around the granola. Spoon your quail's egg yolks out of the soy and in the centre of the beetroot discs. Garnish with micro lemon balm, if available.

Pan-fried Beef Sirloin and Braised Beef Short Rib

These two delicious cuts of beef are served with bone marrow potato purée, teriyaki king oyster mushrooms, crispy shallot rings and a rich beef jus.

Preparation time: 1 hour | Cooking time: 10 hours | Serves 4

Ingredients

For the short ribs
3 beef short ribs (about 2kg)
700g mirepoix root vegetables
6 cloves of garlic, minced
Splash of red wine
2 litres beef stock
Salt and pepper, rapeseed oil

For the potato purée
500g Maris Piper potatoes, peeled and quartered
400g butter
200g double cream (optional)
200g beef bone marrow

For the mushrooms
3 king oyster mushrooms, cleaned and halved lengthways
200ml teriyaki sauce
Knob of butter

For the crispy shallot rings
500ml rapeseed oil
300g shallots, peeled and sliced thinly into rings

For the beef jus
1.5 litres fresh beef stock
½ bottle red wine
200ml Port
100g thyme & 2 star anise

For the sirloin
2 large sirloin steaks
Knob of butter

Method

For the short ribs and bone marrow potato purée
Heat a splash of oil in a large pot on a high heat until it starts to smoke. Fry the ribs, getting an even caramelisation, then remove. Add the mirepoix and fry until golden. Add the garlic and fry for 1 minute, then add a splash of wine to deglaze. Add the ribs back in, cover with stock and cook on a low heat for 8-9 hours, until tender. Once cooked, remove from the liquid (retain 300ml for later) and remove the bone. Cool and place in the fridge. Once cool, cut each bit of meat into a rectangle, then cut in half; you want four equal pieces. Place back in the fridge. Boil the potatoes in salted water until soft, then pass through a potato ricer into a clean pan. Place back on the heat and incorporate the butter until silky smooth. Add the cream if needed. Season.

For the king oyster mushrooms, crispy shallot rings and beef jus
Score the inside of each mushroom, creating a crisscross effect. Brush on the teriyaki sauce. Heat the rapeseed oil in a pan to 135°c. Add handfuls of the shallot rings and deep-fry, stirring continuously, until golden. Remove using a slotted spoon and drain on paper towels. Season with sea salt while hot. In a large saucepan heat the beef stock, red wine and Port on a medium heat. Add the thyme and star anise and reduce. Before it thickens, remove the thyme and star anise. If the sauce over-thickens add some of the reserved cooking liquid from the beef ribs.

To cook
Preheat the oven to 120°c. Place the beef ribs on a tray and cook for 10 minutes, then transfer to a pan with 1 ladle of jus and ½ ladle of beef rib stock. Heat and baste until coated in a nice sticky sauce. Reheat the potato purée. In a frying pan, sauté the bone marrow until tender and mix through the potato purée. Oil and season the steaks and add to a hot frying pan. Cook for 3 minutes, then flip and fry for a further 3. Add a knob of butter and baste for 1 minute. Season and remove from the heat. Wrap the steak in foil and rest for 10 minutes, then cut one in half lengthways and rest again for 3 minutes. Add a little oil to the same pan and fry the mushrooms flat-side down for 2-3 minutes, then flip. Add a knob of butter and baste for a further 2 minutes, or until cooked. Transfer to a tray to keep warm. Place the shallot rings in the oven for 3 minutes prior to plating up. Heat the jus and pour into individual jugs.

To serve
Place the potato purée off-centre, add the steak and top with sea salt. Spoon the beef rib onto the purée, place seven shallot rings on top, and the teriyaki mushroom between the steak and rib. Add the jug of jus to the side.

Dark Chocolate Delice

This elegant dark chocolate delice is accompanied by a mango cremeux, honeycomb pieces, mango and pineapple gel, mango sorbet, white chocolate soil and a raspberry gel.

Preparation time: 2 hours, plus setting and freezing | Serves 4

Ingredients

For the dark chocolate delice
85g bran flakes

100g praline paste & 70ml milk

165ml double cream & 1 egg

170g dark chocolate callets (51%)

50g raspberries, halved, to decorate

For the sorbet & cremeux
60g fructose sugar

250g mango purée

15g lemon juice

½ gelatine leaf & 40ml milk

300ml double cream

17g glucose syrup

250g white chocolate callets

110g mango purée

For the honeycomb
160g caster sugar

60g golden syrup

180g glucose syrup

25g bicarbonate of soda

For the white chocolate soil
100g caster sugar

50g white chocolate callets

For the mango & raspberry gels
100g mango & pineapple purée

Ultratex as required

190g raspberry purée

10g balsamic vinegar

Method

For the dark chocolate delice
Blitz the bran flakes in a food processor, then combine with the praline paste. Divide between four 10 by 4cm moulds (no thicker than a 10p coin) to create the base. Refrigerate. Boil the milk and cream, whisking in the beaten egg as it boils to create a custard. Add the chocolate and let it sit for 1 minute, then whisk until incorporated and thickened. Divide between the four moulds. Set in the freezer.

For the mango sorbet and mango cremeux
Dissolve the fructose sugar with 150ml of water in a saucepan on a high heat. Allow to cool. Once at room temperature, add the mango purée and lemon juice and mix with a stick blender until combined. Add to an ice cream machine and mix until frozen. Freeze. Place the gelatine into a jug of cold water. Mix the milk, cream and glucose syrup together in a saucepan, bring to the boil, then remove from the heat. Add the softened gelatine and stir. Pour the hot liquid over the chocolate and combine with a stick blender. Add the mango purée and mix. Place into the fridge to set, then whip the cremeux using a whisk. Transfer to a piping bag with a 2cm nozzle.

For the honeycomb and white chocolate soil
For the honeycomb, add the caster sugar, golden syrup and glucose syrup to a saucepan with 40ml of water and place on the heat. Heat to 148°c using a sugar thermometer, then whisk in the bicarbonate. Pour the mixture onto a baking sheet and let set. Once set, break into small pieces. For the soil, put the sugar in a pan with 30ml of water and, using a sugar thermometer, heat to 140°c. Add the white chocolate and whisk in until it resembles soil. Transfer to a baking sheet and let cool.

For the gels
Combine the mango purée and the pineapple purée. Add Ultratex, 1 teaspoon at a time, and blend with a stick blender until you reach the desired consistency. Repeat the process with the raspberry purée and balsamic vinegar.

To serve
Turn each delice out 1 hour before serving onto a plate and slice in half lengthways. Once defrosted, pipe three big drops of cremeux on top. Add honeycomb pieces near each drop of cremeux, place a raspberry half against each drop and pipe drops of mango and pineapple gel in the gaps on the top, then repeat with the raspberry gel. Away from the delice, add a tablespoon of white chocolate soil and a scoop of mango sorbet. Pipe more gel around the sorbet and some smaller dots of cremeux.

RECIPES & CHEFS
SEAN 'BADGER' RAINE

Sean 'Badger' Raine

Leading Chef Sean 'Badger' Raine has had a 12-year career in the Royal Navy, which has taken him around the world and seen him take home a silver medal at his first Salon Culinaire.

"I joined the Royal Navy in June 2009. My parents were both in the RAF; John, my Dad, was an RAF Policeman and Terri, my Mam, was a clerk. It was always a long-running family joke that I would get shipped off to Plymouth to join the Navy on my 16th birthday, but my reply was always, "No chance! I'll be in the RAF like you two!" However, when I started looking into careers I was drawn towards the Navy and the unique opportunities it presented.

I wasn't particularly engaged at school – I remember sitting in GCSE maths counting how many words were in particular newspaper articles thinking, what am I doing here? My parents taught me to cook when I was young, so when it came to joining the Navy, I knew straight away that I would choose to go into cooking.

It's definitely been an interesting 12 years so far! My first ship was HMS CORNWALL, a now decommissioned Type 22 frigate. My first deployment saw me travel to the Gulf of Oman as part of CTF 151. The following 4 years were some of the most exciting and expensive to date. They saw me travel all over the world – Australia, Singapore, the Maldives, the Seychelles, the USA, the Caribbean, the list goes on. I spent 69 days straight at sea as part of the search and rescue efforts onboard HMS ECHO looking for the missing Malaysian airline flight 370, which was a challenging task – cooking meals with next to nothing in terms of fresh ingredients.

Subsequent promotion to Leading Chef followed in 2014. After spending 5 years based in Plymouth it was time for a change of scenery. A move to Portsmouth was in order, where an assignment order to HMS DUNCAN arrived in my inbox. I set sail on a 9-month deployment back to the Gulf of Oman. When I returned, I met my now fiancée Aimee on the jetty for the first time in a very romantic moment that would make Hollywood rich! The next four years saw me working with NATO in the Mediterranean and Black Seas, alongside Scott and Mattie, who also feature in this book.

In 2019 my world changed when my son Spencer was born. As my personal needs changed, the Navy changed with me. I moved to HMS MERSEY, a three watch manned ship that allowed me to spend some quality time with our new bundle of joy and nappies, whilst also being able to continue my career.

Recent selection for promotion to Petty Officer Catering Services will see my career continue to progress, and I'm sure I'll visit the remaining parts of the world I've yet to see.

Curried Butternut Squash Soup and Pan-fried Turbot

This warming soup is served with a fillet of turbot, but you could also use salmon, if you prefer.

Preparation time: 20 minutes | Cooking time: 30 minutes | Serves 4

Ingredients

For the soup

1 tbsp vegetable oil

1 white onion, peeled and diced

2 cloves of garlic, finely chopped

1 red chilli, finely diced (or to taste)

1 large butternut squash, peeled, deseeded and diced

1 tsp ground cinnamon

½ tsp ground coriander

2 tbsp curry powder

1 litre good vegetable stock

1½ tbsp brown sugar

1 tbsp natural yoghurt

Salt and pepper

For the fish

1 tbsp vegetable oil

4 x 160-180g fillets of turbot, de-boned

1 large knob of butter

½ lemon, for squeezing

Salt

To serve

Small bunch of watercress

Method

For the soup

In a heavy-bottomed pan, heat the oil over a medium heat. Add the onion, garlic and chilli, and sauté until soft but not browned; roughly 6-7 minutes. Add the butternut squash along with the cinnamon, coriander and curry powder, and sauté for a further 5 minutes. Add the vegetable stock and a pinch of salt, then bring this to the boil. Once boiling, reduce the heat and simmer until the squash is cooked and tender; roughly a further 15 minutes. Once tender, add the sugar and remove from the heat. Purée the soup with a stick blender or in a food processor until smooth. For that extra smooth finish, pour the soup through a sieve to remove any missed bits. Put the soup on a low heat at the back of the stove while you cook the fish.

For the fish

Heat the oil in a large non-stick frying pan over a medium heat. Once the oil is hot, season the fillets of turbot with a little bit of salt and pepper, and place them in the pan skin-side down. This will be the presentation side. Cook until they are golden and crisp on the skin side; roughly 2-3 minutes (tip – press the fillets down with a spatula to help keep the fillets flat whilst the skin crisps up). Turn the fillets over, add a healthy knob of butter and allow this to melt and foam. Spoon the butter over the fish and continue to cook for a further 1-2 minutes, continually basting the fish. Finish with a squeeze of lemon and remove from the heat. To check that the fish is cooked, insert a metal skewer into the thickest part of the fish – it should go through the fish easily and be warm to the touch when removed. If they are particularly thick pieces of fish, or they are left on the bone, you may need to place them in the oven for 4-5 minutes to ensure they are cooked; do this before basting them with butter as the butter may burn if cooked for too long.

To serve

Place a small handful of watercress in a pile in the centre of the bowl, and place your rested piece of fish on top. Stir the yoghurt into the soup, and serve the soup in a jug alongside the plate.

Pan-fried Duck Breast

Here duck breasts are pan-fried to create perfect crispy skin, and served with potato purée, pickled blackberries, duck leg bonbon, peas in a pod and blackberry Port jus.

Preparation time: 30 minutes, plus pickling and chilling | Cooking time: 1 hour 45 minutes | Serves 4

Ingredients

For the pickled blackberries
150g caster sugar & 300ml water
150ml white wine vinegar
5 juniper berries & 1 star anise
Pinch of coriander seeds
Pinch of mustard seeds
Pinch of chilli flakes
250g blackberries

For the jus
2 shallots, finely diced
800ml beef stock
Sprig of rosemary & thyme
50ml Port & 50ml red wine
2 knobs of butter
Salt and pepper

For the bonbons
2 confit duck legs
100g panko breadcrumbs
2 large eggs & 50g flour
500ml vegetable oil

For the potato purée
6-7 Maris Piper potatoes,
peeled and quartered
25ml double cream
25g salted butter

For the duck
4 duck breasts, trimmed
2 tbsp honey

For the peas in a pod
200g peas in a pod

Method

For the pickled blackberries

Add the sugar, vinegar and water to a pan and bring to the boil. As it's warming up, add the dried spices. Once boiling, remove from the heat. Once slightly cooler, add half of the blackberries. Cover and leave to pickle for up to 48 hours.

For the bonbons and jus

For the jus, sauté the shallots with a little oil until soft, add the beef stock and herbs and bring to the boil, then add the remaining blackberries. Reduce the heat and simmer for 1 hour to reduce by half. Add the Port and red wine, and simmer for a further 5-10 minutes. Keep warm. For the bonbons, shred the meat from the bones and mix with the reduced jus, shaping into four ping pong-sized balls. Place these in the fridge for up to 1 hour to set. Whisk the eggs with a tiny pinch of salt. Coat the chilled duck balls first in the flour, then the egg, then the breadcrumbs. Refrigerate.

For the potato purée and bonbons

Boil the potatoes in a pan of salted water for 20-25 minutes. Drain, then allow them to rest and steam for 5 minutes. Mash using a ricer or hand masher until smooth, then add the cream and butter, and mix. Season and keep warm. Preheat the oven to 170°c. To cook the bonbons, place a small pan over a medium heat and fill it three-quarters full with vegetable oil. When the oil is 170°c, fry the bonbons in the oil for 2-3 minutes until golden. Transfer to the oven to keep warm.

For the duck and peas in a pod

Score the skin with a sharp knife in a cross pattern. Place the breasts into a cold frying pan and set over a medium heat. Allow the duck to fry in its own fat until the skin is golden brown and crisp, then turn the duck over and fry for 2-3 minutes more. Once the breast is sealed, transfer to the oven for 5-6 minutes at 170°c, then transfer to a plate with 5-6 sheets of kitchen roll underneath. Brush with the honey and allow to rest for 6-7 minutes under foil. In the frying pan you cooked the duck in, reheat the fat left behind, then add the peas and gently sauté for 2-3 minutes.

To serve

Add the butter to the jus and season. Slice each duck breast diagonally into three slices per person (removing the small top and bottom parts). Place a spoonful of potato to one side of the plate and drag the spoon downwards. Place the bonbon at the thinner end, add the sliced duck to the left and the peas in-between. Dot the blackberries around, then pour a little jus next to the duck.

Pear and Thyme Tarte Tatin with Cinnamon Ice Cream

The delicious homemade ice cream can be made in advance and stored in the freezer, so you only have to worry about the tarte tatin on the day.

Preparation time: 30 minutes, plus freezing | Cooking time: 40 minutes | Serves 4

Ingredients

For the ice cream

300ml full-fat milk

1 tbsp ground cinnamon

1 tsp vanilla extract

150g caster sugar

6 large egg yolks

300ml double cream

For the tarte tatin

1 packet of ready-to-use puff pastry

8 large conference pears

Lemon juice, as needed

75g unsalted butter, cubed

100g golden caster sugar

2 sprigs of thyme, leaves picked

½ tsp cinnamon

Pinch of salt

Method

For the ice cream

Put the milk, cinnamon and vanilla into a saucepan and gently bring to the boil. In a separate mixing bowl, whisk the sugar and egg yolks until pale and fully incorporated. Add the hot milk, whisking constantly. Once fully mixed, transfer this to a fresh, clean saucepan and put it back on the heat. Gently bring back to the boil, stirring constantly. You may feel it beginning to catch on the bottom, but keep going to prevent it curdling or splitting. Once the custard has become thick and coats the back of a wooden spoon, take it off the heat and pour it through a sieve into another clean pan. Allow it to cool. Whip the double cream to soft peaks. Once the custard has sufficiently cooled, add one-third of the whipped cream and mix well. Add the remaining two-thirds gently, being careful not to knock the air out. Transfer to an ice cream machine to churn. If you don't have an ice cream machine, you can put it in the freezer in an airtight container and give it a good whisk every 30 minutes.

For the tarte tatin

Preheat the oven to 200°c. Unroll the puff pastry on a lightly floured surface and roll it to the thickness of a £1 coin. Using a plate that is slightly larger than the top of your tarte tatin dish or frying pan, cut out a circle of pastry. Chill the pastry on a baking tray while you prepare the rest. Peel the pears, cut them in half and scoop out the core. Place them in lemon water until needed. Put the butter in the tarte tatin dish or frying pan along with the sugar, thyme leaves, cinnamon and salt. Gently bring this to the boil and keep an eye on it as it turns to caramel (tip – swirl the pan instead of stirring the caramel). Once a light brown caramel has been achieved, remove the pan from the heat and tightly pack the pears into the pan, overlapping them in a decorative circle. Put the pan back on the heat for 5-10 minutes to begin cooking the pears. The pears will shrink, so if you have a few left over, you can add any remaining pears now. Remove the pan from the heat and leave until cool to the touch. Place the pastry on top and tuck in the edges. Place the pan on a baking tray and bake for 25-30 minutes until the pastry is golden brown. Don't worry if some of the juices come out of the pan. Once cooked, place a serving plate on top and flip the two together to turn the tarte out onto the plate (it may need some light encouragement).

To serve

Place a slice of tarte tatin on a plate and serve with the cinnamon ice cream.

RECIPES
& CHEFS
SIMON MARTIN

Simon Martin

Simon Martin is a talented chef with many strings to his bow. After a 12-year career in the Royal Navy, he has gone on to achieve many accolades and currently heads up the culinary teams for Kerry Taste and Nutrition across the Middle East, Indian sub-continent, Africa and Turkey as Executive Chef.

"Becoming a chef is a story on its own! I left school in the 80s, with dole queues and no qualifications to speak of, so my options were gas fitting or a professional cookery diploma. I think I was actually swayed towards Higbury College (somewhere in later years I would teach), when I discovered that's where they taught air hostesses!

After three years in college I set off towards the bright lights of London to work in the Café Royal, then the famous Langan's Brasserie. One day, after a long shift on the stoves, I was walking home and saw an advert for a sun-drenched beach and had an epiphany… I would join the Royal Navy and become one of those men dressed smartly in white you see on the port, smoking and looking cool.

In 1989 I began a career that would span over 12 years and take me on ships like Ark Royal and to exotic places like Diego Garcia, the Falklands and sunny Belfast. Looking back, it was a blast; the brethren I lived with still support me today and part of me has never left.

Since then I have lived in Moscow, Muscat, Kiev and Dubai. I've run Europe's biggest CUP at Epsom Race Course, been Head Chef at LSG Sky Chefs Heathrow with 200 chefs producing 85,000 meals a day, taught in a college, and, for the past 10 years, created recipes for some of the world's biggest fast food chains.

I'm a Master Craftsman in the Craft Guild of Chefs UK, lead committee member for the Oman Culinary Guild of Chefs, active member of Emirates Culinary Guild, culinary consultant to Saudi Arabian Skills Sector, and question-setter and consultant for City & Guilds of London, as well as culinary advisor to the Universal Infants Free School Meals Initiative for UK.

As well as winning an international gold medal, I have worked alongside chefs such as Yotam Ottolenghi, Alain Ducasse, Gordon Ramsay, Peter Gordon, Mark Hix and Pierre Gagnaire. I have also worked at Presidential functions for the Premiers of Russia, Ukraine, India, the Philippines, South Africa, USA, Malaysia and Saudi Arabia, as well as royals from Thailand, Norway, UK, Kuwait, Saudi Arabia and UAE.

The Middle East is now my home, and my exciting career stemmed entirely from the Royal Navy and the opportunities presented to me there."

Crumpet, Sour Cream and Keta

This dish reflects my time working in Russia and Ukraine. It is indulgent and packed with textures and flavours that will make you crave more with every bite. Soft, fluffy crumpets with a crispy outside, melted butter that enhances the sour cream, then… Pop! The salty burst of the keta… Real posh comfort food.

Preparation time: 30 minutes | Cooking time: 10 minutes | Serves 4 (or 2 if you're as greedy as me!)

Ingredients

For the crumpets

150g plain flour

200ml water

½ tsp salt

1 tsp dried yeast

½ tsp sugar

1 tsp baking powder

To serve

1 red onion, sliced into rings

20g good-quality butter

150g thick sour cream (I love the 20% fat version)

100g keta (salmon or trout roe, jarred or tinned)

Method

First, place the onion rings for serving into some iced water and place in the fridge (covered, so as not to make fridge smell too much).

For the crumpets

In a large bowl whisk the flour, water and salt vigorously (until your arm aches!) and it makes a smooth batter. Mix a few drops of water into the yeast, then add the yeast mixture, sugar and baking powder to the batter and mix again for 1 minute. Cover the bowl and leave in a warm place for 15 minutes until it expands.

Grease four round metal biscuit cutters and place into a non-stick pan over a medium heat. Use a ladle to drop approximately 60g of batter into each ring. After 4 minutes, lift the rings off. If the top seems gooey, flip the crumpets over to cook the second side. Transfer to a cooling rack. Repeat this until all the mixture is consumed .These can be stored for a few days in an airtight container.

To serve

Now for the magic… Place the crumpets in a toaster or under a hot grill until hot and crispy. Butter them while hot – don't skimp! Divide the sour cream on top of the crumpets to create a thick layer; almost half the depth of crumpet. Now spoon on the keta – don't be shy, it should nearly cover the sour cream. Finally, top with a few crispy iced onion rings. Finished!

Mishkaki Prawns, Shirazi Salad and Coconut Tomato Chilli Rice

I've lived in Oman for 5 years, where mishkaki is available on every beach and street corner come dusk. Here it is served with the only rice dish you will ever need to know how to cook (which I adapted from a Nigel Slater recipe), and a shirazi salad on the side.

Preparation time: 30 minutes, plus 2 hours marinating | Cooking time: 30 minutes | Serves 4

Ingredients

For the mishkaki prawns
1 large beef tomato
½ tsp tamarind paste, diluted with 2 tbsp water
2 tbsp vegetable oil
2.5cm ginger, peeled & crushed
2 cloves of garlic, crushed
600g raw peeled king prawns

For the shirazi salad
4 ripe tomatoes, chopped
3 shallots, finely diced
6 radishes, thickly sliced
2 small Lebanese cucumbers, peeled, deseeded and chopped 50g chopped parsley
2 tbsp chopped dill
40g chives, cut into 1.5cm pieces
1 lime, juiced & 2 tbsp olive oil
Edible flowers, to garnish

For the rice
350g basmati rice
2 tbsp vegetable oil
4cm cinnamon stick
12 fresh curry leaves
½ tsp mustard seeds (optional)
½ tsp chipotle flakes
1 large onion, thinly sliced
50g unsalted cashew nuts
1 green chilli, thinly sliced
4 cloves of garlic, crushed
400g tinned tomatoes
400ml tin of coconut milk

Method

For the mishkaki prawns
Place the tomato into a blender and whizz until pulped. Add the tamarind water, oil, ginger and garlic, then season well with salt and pepper. Place the prawns in a zip-lock bag or bowl, add the marinade and leave to marinate for at least 2 hours.

For the shirazi salad
Combine the tomatoes, shallots, radishes, cucumbers, parsley, dill and chives in a bowl. Mix the lime juice, olive oil and a good pinch of salt and pepper to make the dressing. Pour the dressing over the salad and mix together. Place in a serving bowl and top with edible flowers.

For the coconut tomato chilli rice
Rinse the rice until the water runs clear. Heat the oil in a large pan, add the cinnamon, curry leaves, mustard seeds and chipotle flakes, and cook for 1 minute (you will be able to smell the aromas releasing). Add the onion and cook until golden brown and soft. Then add the cashews, chilli and garlic, and cook for a further 2 minutes. Add the tomatoes, put a tight-fitting lid on the pan and cook for 7-8 minutes until the tomatoes become soft and squidgy. Stir in the drained rice and add the coconut milk, a pinch of salt and 200ml of water. Bring to the boil and put the lid on. Don't stir or remove the lid, but turn it down to the lowest heat for 15 minutes. Now comes a test of nerves! Remove it from the heat and let it sit for another 15 minutes.

To serve
Place a skillet or frying pan over a medium heat with a spoonful of oil and wait until the pan starts to smoke, then place the prawns in, being careful as it may spit at you. Cook the prawns for 1-2 minutes on each side, then remove from the heat and leave to rest for 2 minutes. Serve with the rice and salad.

Orange and Olive Oil Cake with Maple Yoghurt

Not overly sweet, but this will work just as well served with a cup of dark roast coffee or a glass of Madeira to finish a meal. I like to use mandarins, but all citrus works, even lemon. Living in the Middle East, I always drizzle mine with a rosewater syrup… so good!

Preparation time: 30 minutes | Cooking time: 35 minutes | Serves 4 (with lots leftover!)

Ingredients

For the cake

4 eggs

3 oranges, zested and juiced

195g olive oil (do not use extra virgin olive oil, as it will overpower the cake)

45g fresh breadcrumbs

100g ground almonds

140g caster sugar

5g baking powder

10ml rosewater syrup (optional)

5g slivered pistachios, to decorate

For the yoghurt

3 tbsp thick Greek yoghurt

2 tbsp maple syrup (or honey, if you prefer)

4 tbsp coconut cream

Method

For the cake

Preheat the oven to 180°c. Grease and line a deep 20cm springform cake tin. Mix the eggs, orange juice and zest, and oil together. In a separate bowl, mix together the breadcrumbs, ground almonds, sugar and baking powder, then slowly add the egg mixture into the dry ingredients. Transfer the cake batter to the lined cake tin and bake in the preheated oven for 30-35 minutes or until a skewer inserted into the cake comes out clean. If using, pour over the rosewater syrup to absorb into the cake. Allow to cool in the tin for at least 20 minutes before taking the cake out to cool completely. It can be made a couple of days in advance.

For the yoghurt

Mix all the ingredients together and chill until needed.

To serve

Warm the cake slightly and serve a generous wedge with a spoonful of the maple and coconut yoghurt on the side, then sprinkle liberally with the slivered pistachios.

RECIPES & CHEFS

SID WILKINS

Sid Wilkins

Over his 30-year career, Simon 'Sid' Wilkins has served on nearly every type of ship in the Royal Navy, cooked for various members of the Royal Family and competed in the Naval Services Culinary Arts Team.

"I joined the Royal Navy straight from school in 1990, but I think I was a chef for about 11 years before I actually started to enjoy it! As I got a bit older and more experienced, I really started to find a passion for cooking. I love Tom Kerridge and his style of cooking, and I always drew inspiration from his recipes. I started competing and moved into fine dining, and this is when I really found my confidence.

I competed as part of the Naval Services Culinary Arts Team, picking up a silver and two golds. I was also lucky enough to cook for more than one Trafalgar Night Dinner on HMS Victory, something that is always an honour. I was the Petty Officer Chef, so was in charge of the menu and bringing the function together.

I have cooked for countless dignitaries, royals and high-ranking officers, especially during my time at Admiralty House, the Naval residence of the Second Sea Lord. One of my funniest memories is coming out to be thanked after cooking a dinner, and a member of the Royal Family speaking to me in an accent so incredibly posh that I had absolutely no idea what he was saying! It was hard to keep a straight face, but it was a real honour nonetheless!

I left the Royal Navy in 2019 after nearly 30 years. I now teach advanced Navy chefs at Worthy Down. I love watching people develop. Sometimes they start like a deer in headlights and I really like seeing their confidence grow as their skills develop. It's quite nice to be able to impart some knowledge – all those little things I've picked up over 30 years that can make your job that little bit easier.

Thinking back, I was always the one in the kitchen that people came to with problems or when they needed help with something. It's nice to know people always saw me as someone they could trust, and I think that's what I enjoy now in my teaching role. I'm looking forward to helping many more young chefs to achieve the best they can over the next few years.

Without the support of my wife, Stephanie, I would not have been able to do all these wonderful things."

Mackerel Tartare with Beetroot and Horseradish

This colourful starter marries the rich flavour of mackerel – which should be as fresh as you can possibly get for best results – with earthy beetroot and a hot yet slightly sweet white chocolate and horseradish soil. The rice cracker is for added texture and the nasturtium oil brightens everything up.

Preparation time: 30 minutes | Cooking time: 2 hours | Serves 4-6

Ingredients

For the white chocolate and horseradish soil
100g caster sugar
50g white chocolate
10g fresh horseradish, grated

For the beetroot gel
500g beetroot
500ml chicken stock
2 tsp balsamic vinegar
15 black peppercorns
1 star anise
1 bay leaf
Pinch of salt
5g agar agar

For the rice cracker
100g white rice

For the nasturtium oil
100g nasturtium leaves
100ml olive oil

For the mackerel tartare
4 mackerel fillets
1 small lemon, zested
1 small shallot, finely diced (2 tsp)
1 tsp finely chopped fresh ginger
2 tsp sea salt
Pinch of black pepper

Method

For the white chocolate and horseradish soil
Bring the sugar and 30ml of water to 136°c in a saucepan. Once the syrup reaches this temperature, add the chocolate and horseradish, and stir until it resembles a crumble. Pour the mixture onto a tray to cool down. Once cooled, it is ready to use.

For the beetroot gel
Peel and slice the beetroot, then combine it with 500ml of water and all the other ingredients except the agar agar in a large saucepan. Bring to the boil, reduce the heat and simmer for 2 hours. Strain the liquid into another pan and reduce it to 500ml, then stir in the agar agar until dissolved. Pour the gel into a bowl to set. Blend the set gel, then pass it through a sieve to get a smooth consistency.

For the rice cracker
Put the rice in a pan with 100ml of water, bring to the boil and simmer until cooked. Drain the rice and spread it over a silicone baking mat (or a baking tray lined with non-stick paper). Place this in the oven to dry out at 80°c for 1 hour. Cut or tear the rice cracker sheet into the required portions, then deep fry them in hot oil until puffed and crispy.

For the nasturtium oil
Blanch the leaves in a pan of boiling water, then transfer them to a blender. Gradually add the oil with the blender running until it reaches the required consistency.

For the mackerel tartare
Skin and dice the mackerel fillets, then combine with all the other ingredients in a bowl, stir gently and leave to marinate for 15 minutes. Taste to check the seasoning, adding more salt or pepper if needed, then it's ready to serve.

To serve
Plate the tartare using food presentation rings, sprinkle the chocolate and horseradish soil around the plate, add dots of beetroot gel and a rice cracker. Finally, drizzle with nasturtium oil and garnish with chive flowers.

Pan-seared Venison Fillet with Truffle Mash

This main course celebrates the very best woodland ingredients. The venison fillet and truffle mash are served with a wild mushroom and pea fricassée, pickled blackberries, a juniper-infused jus and some grated fresh truffle for extra indulgence.

Preparation time: 2 hours | Cooking time: 1 hour | Serves 4-6

Ingredients

For the venison
400g venison fillet

For the pickled blackberries
100ml white wine vinegar
100g caster sugar
1 clove, star anise and bay leaf
5g mustard seeds
200g blackberries

For the juniper-infused jus
175ml Port & 2 tbsp olive oil
4 banana shallots, chopped
10g parsley & 10g thyme
100g juniper berries, crushed
800ml good beef stock
10g dark chocolate
150g unsalted butter

For the truffle mash
1.5kg potatoes, peeled
100-140g butter
300ml full-fat milk, hot
6 tbsp double cream
½ tsp truffle oil & 1 fresh truffle

For the fricassée
40g unsalted butter
30g shallots, chopped
1 clove of garlic, finely chopped
400g wild mushrooms, cleaned
100ml dry white wine
100g petit pois & 10g parsley
15ml lemon juice

Method

For the venison

Trim the venison and remove the sinew, then place on a sheet of cling film and roll up nice and tight, so the venison is round in shape. Place in the fridge until needed.

For the pickled blackberries

Put all ingredients in a pan except the blackberries, bring to the boil and boil for 2 minutes, then strain, keeping the liquor. Cool for 10 minutes, then add the blackberries and leave for at least 2 hours. Drain when ready to serve.

For the juniper-infused jus

Put the olive oil in a frying pan over a medium heat and fry the shallots until golden and caramelised. Add the Port, herbs and juniper, and simmer until reduced by half. Pour in the stock and continue to cook until reduced by half again, then strain. Transfer the sauce into a new pan and bring to the boil, then add the chocolate. Remove from the heat and whisk in the butter, then season with salt, pepper and sugar to taste.

For the truffle mash

Boil the potatoes in salted water until soft. Drain, then return to the pan and cook for 1-2 minutes over a dry heat. Mash thoroughly until lump-free. Gradually beat 100g of the butter into the potato until it starts to look shiny. Heat the milk and cream in a small pan, then mix into the potato purée with salt and pepper. It should become a soft velvety purée. Add the truffle oil and seasoning. Keep warm until required.

For the venison

Preheat the oven to 200°c. Unwrap and sear the venison in a very hot pan, getting a caramelised colour, then put in the oven for 9 minutes. Rest for 18 minutes (covered).

For the fricassée

Put half the butter in a frying pan over a medium heat, add the shallots and soften. Add the finely chopped garlic and the mushrooms, then season. Add the wine, cover and cook for 1-2 minutes, then add the petit pois, lemon juice and remaining butter. Stir and cook for about 5-10 minutes, then add the chopped parsley and season again. Add the truffle mash to the plates and grate over some fresh truffle. Add the rested venison, pickled blackberries, fricassée and jus, as shown in the photo.

Cox's Apple & Thyme Tarte Tatin with Crème Anglaise and Honeycomb

This delicious and classic French dessert is given a lift by the addition of fresh apples and a sprinkle of sea salt to finish the tart. Thyme and apple go really well together, so don't be afraid to give this perfect marriage of sweet and savoury flavours a try.

Preparation time: 15 minutes | Cooking time: 1 hour | Serves 4-6

Ingredients

For the tarte tatin
50g unsalted butter, softened
50g caster sugar
7 Cox's apples
1 sheet of ready-rolled puff pastry

For the crème Anglaise
5 egg yolks
25g caster sugar
200ml cream
280ml milk
1 vanilla pod, halved

For the honeycomb
200g caster sugar
100g golden syrup
2½ tsp bicarbonate of soda

To serve
1 lemon, juiced
Picked thyme leaves
Sea salt

Method

For the tarte tatin
Preheat the oven to 170°c. Place the softened butter into a copper pan and spread it evenly across the base, then sprinkle the sugar over the butter. Peel and halve five of the apples, removing their cores. Place the apple halves on top of the sugar and butter, cut-side down, working outwards from the centre in a fan shape. Lay the pastry over the apples, tucking in the sides between the apple and the pan.
Place the pan on the stove to get the caramel going. Heat just until it's bubbling and golden, then place in a preheated oven to cook for about 1 hour. Turn out the tarte tatin onto a cooling rack, apple-side up. Leave to cool slightly before serving.

For the crème Anglaise
Whisk the egg yolks and sugar together until they are pale and fluffy. Put the cream, milk and split vanilla pod into a pan. Bring the mixture to just before boiling point, then pour it over the egg and sugar mixture while whisking to combine. Pour the crème Anglaise into a clean pan and cook gently, not letting it boil, while stirring until the mixture coats the back of a spoon.

For the honeycomb
Heat the sugar and syrup in a pan until golden, then quickly and thoroughly whisk in the bicarbonate of soda. Pour the frothing mixture onto a silicone mat (or a tray lined with non-stick paper) and leave the honeycomb to cool and set. Break into shards and crush some into dust.

To serve
Peel the remaining two apples and use a melon baller to scoop out small spheres. Put these into a bowl of water mixed with the juice of a lemon, then roll them in the honeycomb dust just before serving with the tarte tatin, honeycomb and crème Anglaise. Finish with some of the caramel from the pan, some picked thyme leaves and sea salt.

RECIPES & CHEFS

STEPHEN BENN

Stephen Benn

Ex-CPOCS Stephen Benn served for a number of years before leaving the
Royal Navy to pursue his culinary expertise with Compass UK & Ireland,
competing at an international level on the world stage.

"I joined the Navy in 1990, initially training at HMS Raleigh then moving on to the cookery school in Aldershot before joining HMS Sultan in 1991. I got married and had kids quite young, so lots of my time was spent with them, but I did develop a real interest in cheffing while on my first ship, HMS Invincible. I was working in the officer's mess under one of the chief cooks who was very much a desserts and pastry man, leading me to discover how much I enjoyed that side of the kitchen.

Following a couple of moves to Scotland and back again, I went on a leading chefs qualifying course in 1999. This was a turning point because it brought back my passion and flair for cooking. Rod Naylor was one of the instructors, an influential chef for chocolate and desserts, which really inspired me. The next stage of my career involved promotion to Petty Officer and time in the submarine service, but the strain of being away was hitting my family hard and it was a difficult time personally.

I reached another turning point in 2008 when John Potts, one of the chefs from HMS Illustrious, created a team of chefs to compete at the Scottish culinary championships in Glasgow. The experience gave me back what I had been missing, and afterwards I put together a joint team of military and civilian chefs/stewards from HMNB Clyde including Fraser Mcintosh and Susan Morris to compete at Exercise Joint Caterer. It had never been done before and they did fantastically well. My final posting to HMS Dauntless gave me the opportunity to get back into the kitchen, cooking for dinner parties and events, before I was retired after my 22 years of service.

Knowing I still had a lot to give, I started working with ESS Support Services Worldwide, part of Compass Group, the very next day as a chef manager. This has enabled me to compete again, to further my passion for floral sugarcraft, to learn from inspirational chefs including Willie Pike and Graham Singer, and even to judge a competition at the City of Glasgow College. I've also remarried; my wife June is so supportive of my career and my sons, one of whom now lives with us and is a chef himself. I've had some real ups and downs with some incredible career milestones along the way, and I'm lucky to be involved with the great culinary team at Compass Group."

Pan Seared Fillet of Sea Bass

This recipe celebrates sea bass, which is one of the finest fish in the sea with its silver-coloured skin and superb flavour. I've served it with some fine Scottish langoustine tails, lightly spiced couscous, gingered baby gem and a chilli and sweetcorn salsa.

Preparation time: 45 minutes | Cooking time: 30 minutes | Serves 4

Ingredients

4 x 120g portions of fresh sea bass fillet

Salt and mill pepper

½ lemon, juiced

30g butter

For the langoustine

50g each plain flour & cornflour

½ tsp baking powder

2g salt

175ml sparkling water, chilled

4 langoustine tails

For the gingered baby gems

100g baby gem leaves, washed

25ml honey

20ml soy sauce

10g pickled pink ginger, shredded with a knife

For the sweetcorn salsa

100g tinned or frozen sweetcorn kernels

15ml vegetable oil

½ red, green and yellow pepper

½ red onion

1 tomato, blanched and skinned

1 spring onion, sliced

½ lime, juiced

30ml sweet chilli sauce

5g fresh coriander, chopped

Method

Trim the sea bass fillet and score the skin a few times. Season both sides with a little salt and mill pepper. Heat a little vegetable oil in a frying pan and add the sea bass fillet skin side down. Cook for 2 to 3 minutes until the skin is crisp. Spoon over a little lemon juice and add the butter. Turn the fish over and gently finish the cooking.

For the langoustine

Sieve the flours, baking powder and salt into a bowl, then stir in the chilled sparkling water to make a thin batter. Pull the langoustine tails through the batter, then carefully deep fry them in hot oil at 180°c until crisp and golden. Place on absorbent paper to drain and allow to rest before serving.

For the gingered baby gems

Place the baby gems in a frying pan and add the remaining ingredients. Cover with a lid and cook for 4 to 5 minutes. Serve hot.

For the sweetcorn salsa

Drain the sweetcorn and pat dry with a clean tea towel. Heat the vegetable oil in a pan until smoking, then add the sweetcorn and brown all over. Tip into a tray to cool. Meanwhile, neatly dice all the peppers and finely chop the red onion. Remove the seeds from the tomato and dice the flesh. Whisk the lime juice and sweet chilli sauce together in a bowl, then add the chopped coriander and season the dressing to taste. Mix the dressing with the sweetcorn, peppers, tomato, red onion and spring onion, then allow to infuse before serving.

To serve

I like to prepare some couscous, cooked according to the instructions on the packet with either chicken or vegetable stock, and mixed with some sautéed Mediterranean vegetables, spices such as cumin and coriander, toasted pine nuts and a lemon and honey dressing.

Place a spoonful of the spiced vegetable couscous in the middle of the plate. Top with a gingered baby gem and a portion of cooked sea bass. Surround this with sweetcorn salsa, adding some more toasted pine nuts and a drizzle of lemon and honey dressing if you like. Finally, garnish your starter with the langoustine tempura.

Boudin of Quail and Stornoway Black Pudding

Boudin means 'blood sausage' in French, so this version uses award-winning black pudding to stuff the quail breast. It's served with a savoury thyme pancake, caramelised apples, truffled spinach and a sauce made with the quail bones and finished with Calvados.

Preparation time: approx. 1 hour | Cooking time: approx. 1 hour | Serves 4

Ingredients

4 whole quail
100g Stornoway black pudding
Salt and ground black pepper

For the sauce

1 tbsp olive oil
60g each carrot & celery, diced
80g onion, diced
1 clove of garlic
50g tomato flesh, diced
100ml red wine
Sprig of thyme
200ml double chicken stock
20g foie gras butter

For the pancake

100ml milk
15g beaten egg
1 tsp melted butter
60g plain flour
½ tsp baking powder
½ tsp chopped fresh thyme

For the caramelised apple

2 Granny Smith apples, peeled
50g caster sugar
20ml Calvados

For the truffled spinach

10ml truffle oil
100g spinach leaves, washed
1 whole nutmeg

Method

Cut an incision down the back of the quail and gently remove the skin, keeping it intact. Remove both the legs, the wishbone and the breasts. Chop up the carcass and the legs for the sauce. Lay the skin out on cling film and season with salt and a little truffle oil. Place a quail breast on the skin and add a quarter of the black pudding. Place the inner fillets on either side and top with the other breast. Repeat with all the quail and black pudding. Fold over the skin and roll up to form a cylinder, then tie the cling film tightly at each end. Chill. To cook the boudin, poach in chicken stock for about 6 minutes and sear in a hot frying pan until coloured.

For the sauce

Place the quail legs and carcasses in a roasting tin and cook in the oven at 230°c for 30 to 45 minutes until golden brown, turning a few times. Heat the oil in a large pan and brown the diced vegetables and garlic until caramelised, then add the tomato and red wine. Cook until the wine has almost evaporated, then add the roasted bones, thyme and chicken stock. Bring to the boil, skim the surface and simmer. Strain the sauce, add a little Calvados to taste, then stir in the foie gras butter.

For the pancake

Combine the milk, egg and melted butter then whisk in the flour, baking powder and thyme. Season. Heat a little oil in a non-stick pan, spoon in the pancake mixture and cook for 2 minutes before flipping to finish cooking on the other side.

For the caramelised apple

If you have one, use a parisienne scoop to create balls of apple, or cut into slices. Heat the sugar in a dry pan until it melts and starts to turn golden, then add the apples and Calvados. Stir to combine and coat the apple, then set aside to cool.

For the truffled spinach

Heat the truffle oil in a pan, add the spinach and cook for 10 seconds. Season with salt, pepper and grated nutmeg to taste, then drain off any excess liquid.

To serve

Place the warm pancake on a plate, top with the truffled spinach and the boudin, spoon the apples and caramel around the edge, then finish with the sauce. Garnish with chervil if you like.

Pineapple Tarte Tatin

This recipe was written for the 2010 Exercise Joint Caterer Cook and Serve Competition. It brings together some fantastic flavours in the tarte tatin, passionfruit soufflé and exotic fruit salad. It's served with a coconut and lemongrass ice cream, but you can use a good-quality shop-bought coconut ice cream here, rather than face the complexities of making your own!

Preparation time: 1 hour | Cooking time: 25 minutes | Serves 4

Ingredients

For the tarte tatin

4 sheets of ready-made all-butter puff pastry
1 pineapple
100g caster sugar
50g unsalted butter, cubed
Icing sugar, for dusting

For the soufflé

Melted butter, for greasing
1 level tsp pectin powder
100ml passionfruit purée
100g egg white
20g caster sugar

For the fruit salad

50g sugar
100ml water
1 lime, zested
¼ red chilli, finely chopped
Tabasco, to taste
1 mango
1 pineapple
1 kiwi fruit

Method

For the tarte tatin

Roll the puff pastry out to a thickness of about 2mm, then cut out four circles about 10cm in diameter. To prepare the pineapple, remove the skin and any eyes, quarter and core it, then slice the fruit into even pieces. Pat dry to remove excess moisture. Make a direct caramel by heating a pan on the stove and gently melting the caster sugar, using a spoon to ensure it melts and colours evenly, until it becomes a light golden caramel. Remove from the heat and add the cubed butter, stirring until incorporated. Pour a thin layer of caramel on the base of each tatin pan or individual foil dishes. Place the sliced pineapple on top of the caramel, then drape a circle of pastry over the top and tuck it in well around the edges to completely encase the fruit. Place the tarts on a tray in a preheated oven at 220°c to cook for 18 to 20 minutes, or until the pastry is golden brown. Remove from the oven and rest for 1 minute to let the caramel cool and set slightly before turning out.

For the soufflé

Prepare the ramekins by brushing the bases and up the sides with melted butter. Fill them with caster sugar and empty out so only a thin coating is left. Add the pectin to the passionfruit purée in a small pan and bring to the boil while whisking continuously. When this mixture is jam-like, pour it through a sieve into a bowl and set aside. Whisk the egg whites and caster sugar together until stiff. Fold the meringue mixture through the warm purée in three stages and incorporate well. Spoon into prepared moulds and level the surface. Bake in a preheated oven at 175°c for approximately 6 minutes and serve immediately.

For the fruit salad

Make a stock syrup by bringing the sugar and water to the boil in a small pan. Add the finely chopped chilli and lime zest, cover with cling film and allow to cool. Stir in a few drops of Tabasco to taste. Neatly dice the fruits and place them in a bowl, then pour over the chilled syrup and allow to infuse before serving.

To serve

Carefully turn your tarte tatin onto a warm plate and lift away the tin, drizzling any remaining caramel over and around the tart. Place your soufflé and a quenelle of ice cream on the plate, then spoon on the fruit salad along with some of the syrup.

RECIPES
& CHEFS
TOM
'JULES'
ANDREWS

Tom 'Jules' Andrews

Tom Andrews, or Jules as he is known, has spent over a decade within the Royal Navy. From cooking on submarines to competing in the USA, Jules has pushed himself to excel in everything he has done.

"Even though I am from a military family, being a chef was always my career goal, long before wanting to join the military. I remember a time when I was about six, helping my mum while she was baking biscuits and cakes, and I loved it. She even bought me a toy kitchen set, although that was probably just to keep me out of the way! She wasn't especially in love with cooking, but she instilled a real love for food in me from a young age – particularly with pastry, cakes and desserts, which led me down the path of training to become a pastry chef.

I joined the Royal Navy in 2010 just after I turned 17 and immediately opted for further training to join the Submarine Service. The Navy seemed a better option for me, because, as a chef, I didn't want to be left out of the action back in the camp kitchen! I spent the next seven years on Hunter Killer submarines, which was a highly challenging and highly secretive experience.

Early in my career I was selected to join the Royal Navy Culinary Arts Team, where my passion for fine food was sparked and nurtured by some fantastic mentors (some of whom are also in this book!) who gave me some huge, once-in-a-lifetime opportunities, like representing the Royal Navy in competition with the USA, and training directly under the Royal Pastry

Chef at Buckingham Palace. I was later selected for the Combined Services Culinary Arts Team and given the huge honour of representing the United Kingdom at the 2020 Culinary Olympics in Stuttgart.

In 2018, I joined the Aircraft Carrier HMS Queen Elizabeth, and over my 2 years onboard, completed the roles of Forward Galley Assistant Manager, responsible for feeding up to 1000 people at a time; Commanding Officer's Chef, responsible for feeding the Captain and any VIP Guests; and as Head Baker, taking charge of all the bread and desserts for 1500 people on board. That's a lot of baking – we were getting through 32kg of flour a day!

Desserts are by far my favourite thing to make, I love them. It brings back those early childhood memories of jelly, custard and cake that would always make me and my brothers so happy.

I am currently a Divisional Leading Hand Instructor at HMS Raleigh, instructing the brand-new recruits into the Royal Navy: turning civilians into sailors. I'm super excited for new challenges ahead, including competing in the 2022 Culinary World Cup in Luxembourg. It's been such an honour to have all these opportunities and so many still to come."

Ham Terrine with Pease Pudding

A cold starter is always a good option for a dinner party; it relieves the pressure of having to cook two hot courses, and you can focus on getting everything perfect. This terrine needs to be made the day before being served, but it's definitely worth the wait.

Preparation time: 6 hours + | Cooking time: 2-2.5 hours | Serves 4-6

Ingredients

For the terrine

1 large ham hock
Handful of peppercorns
4 bay leaves
1 bulb of garlic, split
5 pickled gherkins, chopped
Handful of chopped parsley
Salt and pepper
Pea shoots, to garnish (optional)
Toasted crusty bread, to serve

For the pease pudding

2 tbsp vegetable oil
1 small white onion, chopped
1 small carrot, chopped
150g yellow split peas
Few sprigs of rosemary & thyme
40g salted butter
Salt and pepper

For the red pepper ketchup

2 large red peppers, quartered, seeds and pith removed
1 tbsp vegetable oil
1 small red onion, finely chopped
1 clove of garlic, minced
1 tbsp red wine vinegar
2 tbsp brown sugar
1 tbsp tomato purée
Salt and pepper

Method

For the terrine

Place the ham hock, peppercorns, bay leaves and split garlic into a large pot and cover with cold water. Gently bring to the boil and simmer for 2-2½ hours. Remove the ham hock and leave to cool. Strain the cooking liquid into a clean pan and simmer again until it has reduced by two thirds. Shred the ham hock and discard any sinew or skin. Mix the finely chopped gherkins in with the hock, along with a few tablespoons of the reduced liquid, the chopped parsley, and some salt and pepper. Press the meat firmly into individual rings (tuna cans with the tops and bottoms removed are great for this!), spoon a little more of the reduced liquid into the rings and compress in the fridge overnight.

For the pease pudding

Heat the vegetable oil in a medium saucepan and add the onion and carrot. Gently sauté until soft but not brown. Add the yellow split peas, rosemary, thyme and 1 litre of water (or enough to cover the peas), then bring to the boil, skim off any foam and reduce to a low simmer until the peas are soft and tender (approximately 2½ hours). Strain, discard the herbs and blend until smooth. Stir in the butter and season with salt and pepper to taste. Leave to cool completely.

For the red pepper ketchup

Place the pepper quarters onto a baking tray, skin-side up, and place under a hot grill until the skins blacken. Cover with cling film and leave to cool. Peel, discard the skins and chop the pepper flesh. Heat the oil in a saucepan and sweat the onion and garlic in the hot oil until soft but not brown. Add the red pepper, vinegar and brown sugar, and gently simmer for 2-3 minutes until the sugar has dissolved. Add the tomato purée and blend until smooth. Season to taste with salt and pepper. Chill and place into a squeezy bottle or piping bag.

To serve

30-40 minutes before serving, push the terrines out of their ring moulds onto serving plates. When ready to serve, use two spoons to mould a neat quenelle of pease pudding on top of the terrine and squeeze a generous amount of red pepper ketchup around the plate. Garnish with pea shoots, and serve with a slice of good-quality, toasted crusty bread.

Pan-roasted Chicken with Confit Leg Bonbons

The humble chicken is often overlooked when it comes to finer food, but if you prepare and cook it properly, it can be truly delicious. This recipe also utilises the whole bird, with the bones and carcass used to make a delicious sauce, so not a scrap goes to waste.

Preparation time: 24 hours | Cooking time: 10 hours | Serves 4

Ingredients

For the chicken and sauce
2 organic whole chickens
2 celery sticks, roughly chopped
2 carrots, roughly chopped
1 large onion, roughly chopped
Handful of chestnut mushrooms
Handful of parsley stalks
4 bay leaves & 10 peppercorns
100ml white wine
80ml double cream

For the pan-roasted breasts
200g salt & 180g sugar
Vegetable oil, for frying

For the confit leg bonbons
600g salted butter, diced
6 cloves of garlic, crushed
Few sprigs of rosemary & thyme
150g seasoned flour
2 eggs & 200g breadcrumbs
800ml vegetable oil

For the chive creamed potato
600g Russet/Yukon Gold potatoes
2 cloves of garlic, crushed
60g salted butter
50ml double cream
Handful of chopped chives

For the green peas
80g pork lardons
1 shallot, finely diced
300g shelled garden peas

Method

For the chicken and sauce
Joint the chickens into breasts, legs and wings, and reserve the carcasses. Set aside the breasts, legs and wings for later. Place the chicken carcasses and roughly chopped vegetables into roasting trays and roast at 160°c until brown. Place everything into a large pot, and thoroughly deglaze the trays with water. Add the mushrooms, parsley, bay leaves, peppercorns and enough water to cover the bones, and simmer gently for 8 hours; do not stir. Strain through a fine sieve into a clean pan and gently reduce by two thirds, skimming off any grease. In a separate pan, reduce the white wine by half, then add to the stock, along with the cream. Season and keep warm until ready.

For the pan-roasted breasts
Preheat the oven to 160°c. Dissolve the salt and sugar in 2 litres of water. Add the chicken breasts. Cover and refrigerate overnight. 2 hours before cooking, rinse the chicken and pat dry. Heat a large oven-safe skillet with a little vegetable oil. Add the chicken breasts, skin-side down, and cook until golden brown, then turn skin-side up, transfer to the oven and roast for 20 minutes, or until the juices run clear. Rest.

For the confit leg bonbons
Preheat the oven to 130°c. Place the chicken legs, wings, butter, garlic and herbs into a roasting dish and cook for 3 hours. Remove the chicken and cool before picking the meat away from the bones (reserve a cleaned wing bone for each bonbon). Season and roll into ping pong-sized balls. Roll each ball in the seasoned flour, then dip in the egg and finally coat in the breadcrumbs. Heat 5cm depth of vegetable oil in a saucepan or deep fryer to 180°c, then deep-fry the bonbons until golden brown.

For the chive creamed potato and green peas with lardons
Boil the potatoes and crushed garlic in water until soft. Strain and pass through a potato ricer or sieve. Beat in the butter, cream and chives, and season. Keep warm, and place in a piping bag just before service. Add the lardons to a cold, dry frying pan and heat. Once slightly crispy, add the chopped shallot and sauté for 2 minutes. Add the peas, reduce the heat and cook gently until the peas are tender. Season.

To serve
Place the breast on the plate and pipe a generous mound of potato next to it. Chop one end of the reserved wing bone off, and stick the longer half into the bonbon like a lollipop and place on the opposite end of the breast. Spoon the peas in between and ladle the sauce over the breast and around the plate.

Rich Chocolate and Raspberry Tart

Deceptively simple to make, this rich, indulgent tart is deeply chocolatey but perfectly balanced with the sour raspberry gel and is guaranteed to make any chocoholic's day. If ever the Captain had a surprise lunch or dinner party onboard, I'd make this and it would never disappoint.

Preparation time: 30 minutes, plus 3-4 hours chilling | Cooking time: 15-20 minutes | Serves 10-12

Ingredients

For the pastry
240g plain flour
60g icing sugar
120g cold unsalted butter, diced, plus extra for greasing
1 medium egg
½ tsp vanilla paste

For the raspberry gel
250g raspberries, plus extra to decorate
100ml apple juice (fresh if possible)
30g icing sugar
10g cornflour

For the chocolate filling
350g 54% dark chocolate
350g double cream

For the decoration (optional)
Freeze-dried raspberry powder (available at most health food shops or online)
Sprigs of lemon balm

Method

For the pastry

Sift the flour and icing sugar into the bowl of a stand mixer with a paddle attachment. Add the diced butter and mix slowly until the mixture resembles fine breadcrumbs. Alternatively, rub the butter into the flour with your fingertips. Beat the egg with the vanilla paste, then slowly pour into the bowl while mixing until a smooth dough is formed. Flatten the pastry into a disc, wrap in cling film and rest in the fridge for 30 minutes. Preheat the oven to 160°c and lightly grease a 23 by 3cm loose-bottomed tart ring. Roll out the pastry on a lightly floured surface to the thickness of a pound coin. Gently place it into the greased tart ring and push tightly into the corners, with the edges overhanging. Prick the pastry case with a fork, then cover with baking parchment and baking beans and blind bake in the preheated oven for 10 minutes. Uncover the pastry and bake again for another 5 minutes, or until the centre is pale golden. Leave to cool at room temperature, then trim off the excess pastry.

For the raspberry gel

Blend the raspberries, apple juice and icing sugar in a food processor until smooth. Pass the mixture through a fine sieve, then warm it in a small saucepan. Mix a few drops of water or apple juice into the cornflour to make a loose paste. Stir this into the warmed raspberry juice. Gently bring the mixture to the boil, stirring continuously, until the mixture is thick and glossy. Allow to cool, then refrigerate until completely chilled. One chilled, beat the gel thoroughly until smooth, then pass it through a fine sieve into a piping bag or squeezy bottle. Keep in the fridge until serving.

For the chocolate filling

Break the chocolate into small chunks and place in a large heatproof bowl. Warm the double cream in a pan over a medium heat until just below boiling point, then pour the cream over the chocolate and stir until melted and fully incorporated. Pour the mixture into the tart case and leave to set in the fridge for 2 hours.

To serve

Once the filling is completely set, it's time to decorate. Dust the top of the tart with freeze-dried raspberry powder and pipe blobs of the raspberry gel on top. Slice the extra raspberries and decorate the edge of the tart with them. Finish with small sprigs of lemon balm.